Facing History and Ourselves uses lessons of history to challenge teachers and their students to stand up to bigotry and hate. For more information about Facing History and Ourselves, please visit our website at www.facinghistory.org.

Reprinted September 2021.
Last updated October 2023

ISBN-13: 978-1-940457-38-3

ACKNOWLEDGMENTS

We would like to thank the following individuals and organizations for making possible the creation of this curriculum and professional development for Chicago Public Schools*:

Anonymous (2)
Aon Foundation
The Baskin Family Foundation
Christopher Family Foundation
The Crown Family
Karen Harrison and Walter Freedman
Jackson
Robert R. McCormick Foundation
Linda and Judd Miner
Oppenheimer Family Foundation
PPM America
Pritzker Pucker Family Foundation
The Segal Family Foundation
The Charles & M.R. Shapiro Foundation
Jill Garling and Tom Wilson
Zell Family Foundation

*Recognizing commitments made as of August 2021.

CONTENTS

PART 4: THE NATIONAL SOCIALIST REVOLUTION

PART 5: CONFORMITY AND CONSENT IN THE NATIONAL COMMUNITY

PART 6: OPEN AGGRESSION AND WORLD RESPONSE

PART 7: THE HOLOCAUST

PART 8: LEGACIES AND PARTICIPATION

SHARING OUR LEARNING: WRITING CONNECTIONS

WHAT IS FACING HISTORY & OURSELVES?

Facing History & Ourselves is an international educational and professional development organization whose mission is to use lessons of history to challenge teachers and their students to stand up to bigotry and hate. For more information about Facing History & Ourselves, please visit our website at www.facinghistory.org.

WHAT IS THE FACING HISTORY SCOPE AND SEQUENCE?

While every Facing History class is unique, each is organized to follow our scope and sequence, which we often call the Facing History journey. The journey begins by examining common human behaviors, beliefs, and attitudes you can readily observe in your own life. Then, we explore a historical case study and analyze how those patterns of human behavior may have influenced the choices individuals made in the past—to participate, stand by, or stand up—in the face of injustice. Finally, we examine how the history you studied continues to influence our world today, and consider how you might choose to participate in bringing about a more humane, just, and compassionate world.

WHAT WILL YOU LEARN IN THIS UNIT?

Part 1: Introducing the Unit. Prior to exploring the historical case study of this unit—the collapse of democracy in Germany and the steps leading up to the Holocaust—you will spend some time establishing and nurturing classroom rules and expectations of respect and open-mindedness.

Part 2: Identity and Belonging. Who am I? Who are you? Who are we? Who are "they"? How we answer these questions shapes how we think about, and how we behave toward, ourselves and others. And our answers to those questions are influenced by the society we live in. This section explores the relationship between the individual and society, and how that relationship affects who we choose to include in our universe of obligation.

Part 3: The Weimar Republic. The Weimar Republic, the post–World War I German government named for the German city where it was formed, lasted more than 14 years, but democracy never found firm footing. This section explores Germany in the years preceding the Nazis' ascension to power by highlighting efforts to turn a fledgling republic into a strong democracy and examining the misunderstandings, myths, and fears that often undercut those efforts.

Part 4: The National Socialist Revolution. On January 30, 1933, President Paul von Hindenburg named Adolf Hitler chancellor of Germany. Within days of Hitler's appointment, the Nazis began to target their political opposition and those they considered enemies of the state, especially Communists and Jews. Within months, they had transformed Germany into a dictatorship. This section chronicles the National Socialist revolution that swept through Germany in 1933, and it examines the choices individual Germans were forced to confront as a result.

Part 5: Conformity and Consent in the National Community. By 1934, Hitler considered the National Socialist revolution in Germany complete. In control of the nation, the Nazis turned their attention to creating a racially pure "national community" in which Nazism was not revolutionary but normal. This section focuses on the methods the Nazis used to get individuals to conform, if not consent, to their vision for German society. It also focuses on the consequences faced by those who did not fit into the "national community" the Nazis envisioned.

Part 6: Open Aggression and World Responses. Between 1935 and 1939, Nazi Germany began taking aggressive steps toward rebuilding the German military and expanding the Third Reich across Europe. At the same time, Nazi hostility toward Jews within the Reich intensified, culminating in the 1938 pogroms known as Kristallnacht. This section explores the open aggression of Nazi Germany in the late 1930s toward both neighboring countries and individuals within its borders, as well as the dilemmas faced by leaders around the world in response.

Part 7: The Holocaust. As the Third Reich reached the height of its power in Europe, the Nazis began to murder unfathomable numbers of Jews and others of so-called inferior races. This section examines events and human behavior that both unsettle us and elude our attempts to explain them. The resources force us to confront the shocking violence of the Holocaust and reflect on the range of human behavior revealed in the choices of perpetrators, bystanders, resisters, and rescuers.

Part 8: Legacies and Participation. The Holocaust and World War II left profound legacies—in the shape of the immediate aftermath of the war and the decades that followed, in the lives of individuals and the course of nations, and in the new ideas, laws, policies, and institutions that were developed in response to the death and destruction.

HOW SHOULD YOU PREPARE FOR THE UNIT?

Contracting

Throughout this unit, you will engage in discussions that may spark powerful emotions, and you will examine sources that depict racism and violence. When you create a class contract at the beginning of the unit, your teacher will ask you about what you will need to have these discussions. Consider what helps you learn and take care of yourself. What might you add to the contract about what you need from your teacher and classmates? For example, you may want to include that you can choose to reflect privately in a journal instead of with a partner.

Checking in with Your People

We also invite you to check in regularly with trusted people in your life about your learning. You can use the following questions as a starting point for these conversations:

- How are you feeling about what you learned today?
- Was there a discussion, primary source reading, or a moment in class today that stood out to you? Why do you think it caught your attention?
- Is there anything you learned today that you find surprising? Or troubling? Why?
- What questions do you have about what you are learning that you might want to explore more?

Note about Emotionally Challenging Content and Dehumanizing Language

This unit uses historical descriptions and firsthand accounts that depict violent or disturbing events as well as racist and dehumanizing language. Before you read a source with racist or dehumanizing language, your teacher will remind you about the impact that this language can have and that it will not be read aloud. Remember that you can talk to your teacher, or other people in your life that you trust, about what you are thinking and feeling as you process these sources. You can also talk to your teacher about your classroom contract, opportunities for journaling and remember to check in with your people about what you are thinking and feeling.

HOW WILL YOU SHARE WHAT YOU LEARN?

Assessment: At the end of the unit, you will complete a summative performance task that has two parts: a writing prompt and an informed action. For the writing prompt, you will write an essay with an argument that addresses the essential question using specific claims and relevant evidence from historical and contemporary sources while acknowledging competing views.

In the performance task you will apply lessons gained from your study of the Holocaust to your own communities. The informed action has three parts:

1. **UNDERSTAND:** In groups of three to five, you will research the universal rights and responsibilities in the Universal Declaration of Human Rights (UDHR), which arose, in part, as an effort to prevent another global calamity on the scale of the Holocaust.
2. **ASSESS:** In the same groups you will, consider how the UDHR applies to your community (e.g., your school, neighborhood, or some other community to which you belong). You will pick a right from the UDHR that you believe is particularly meaningful and/or not fully achieved in your community. Then you will:
    - Identify a group or individual who has power over addressing the human right that you identify (e.g., your peers, the media, elected officials, nonprofit organizations)
    - Determine what message you think they most need to hear related to the UDHR/your identified issue
    - Decide on a medium to effectively communicate your message to your intended audience
3. **ACT:** You will disseminate your group's chosen right through a medium of your choice (e.g., a mini-exhibition, mural, video documentary, podcast, zine, spoken word poem, or blog post). Be sure to illustrate or explain why that right has particular resonance for your community. In addition, your medium and message should be tailored to appeal to an individual or group with power over your chosen issue.

LETTER TO STUDENT

Dear student,

Welcome. You are about to begin a unit of study created by our organization, Facing History & Ourselves. Facing History's mission is to use lessons of history to challenge teachers and their students (you!) to stand up to bigotry and hate. While you study this history, you will be exploring questions about yourself and your responsibility to others in the world around you. That is what we mean by "facing history and ourselves."

A former Facing History student explained, "When I took the Facing History course back in eighth grade, it helped me understand that history was a part of me and that I was a part of history. If I understood why people made the choices they did, I could better understand how I make choices and hopefully make the right ones."

This unit may be different from others you have experienced. It will ask you to explore questions such as: *Who am I? What shapes who I am becoming? Why do people form groups? What does it mean to belong? What happens when people are excluded?* And it will ask you to consider these questions through the lens of history, exploring the decisions people made in the past, and the impact they have had on our world today. Although one person's choices may not seem important at the time, little by little, they define who we are as individuals, communities, and ultimately, as a nation.

This unit will ask you to use both your head and your heart to make sense of the choices people made in the past and the choices they continue to make today. You will be asked to listen carefully to the voices of others and may engage in discussions and with content that spark powerful emotions. It's important to process what you learn and take care of yourself, by journaling and talking with your classmates, teachers, and caregivers. By working together and supporting one another, we create a classroom where everyone can do their best learning.

We wish you a meaningful journey during which you engage in learning about the past and the present, about yourself, and about others.

Facing History & Ourselves

HANDOUT

CLASSROOM EXPERIENCE CHECKLIST

DIRECTIONS: **Check the box that best matches your experience as a student.**

PART 1

As a student in a classroom, have you ever . . .

1. Shared an idea or question out loud? ☐ Yes ☐ No
2. Shared an idea or question that you thought might be unpopular or "stupid"? ☐ Yes ☐ No
3. Had an idea or answer to a question but decided not to share it? ☐ Yes ☐ No
4. Felt "put down" after sharing an idea or asking a question? ☐ Yes ☐ No
5. Felt smart or appreciated after sharing an idea or asking a question? ☐ Yes ☐ No
6. Asked for help in understanding something? ☐ Yes ☐ No
7. Been confused but have not asked for help? ☐ Yes ☐ No
8. Interrupted others when they have been speaking? ☐ Yes ☐ No
9. Been interrupted by others when you have been speaking? ☐ Yes ☐ No
10. Said something that you thought might have hurt someone's feelings? ☐ Yes ☐ No
11. Thought of your classroom as a community? ☐ Yes ☐ No

PART 2

What do you think should happen in a classroom in order for the best learning to take place?

What can students do to support your learning and each other's learning?

HANDOUT

SAMPLE FACING HISTORY CLASSROOM EXPECTATIONS

- Listen with respect. Try to understand what someone is saying before rushing to judgment.

- Make comments using "I" statements.

- This class needs to be a place where we can take risks in the questions we ask, perspectives we share, and connections we make. If you do not feel safe making a comment or asking a question, write the thought in your journal. You can share the idea with your teacher first and together come up with a safe way to share the idea with the class.

- If someone says something that hurts or offends you, do not attack the person. Acknowledge that the comment—not the person—hurt your feelings and explain why.

- Share the talking time—provide room for others to speak.

- We all have a role in creating a space where people can share their ideas, their questions, and their confusion honestly.

HANDOUT

WRITING PROMPT

DIRECTIONS:

- Circle words you do not know or understand in the context of the prompt.
- Star words that seem to be the central ideas of the prompt.
- Underline all of the verbs that represent what you, as the writer, are supposed to do.
- Cross out any information that does not seem specifically relevant to the writing task.

How did the choices of individuals, groups, and nations lead to the Holocaust?

In an essay, construct an argument that addresses this question using specific claims and relevant evidence from historical and contemporary sources while acknowledging competing views.

READING

WORDS MATTER

How does it feel to be called by a name you did not choose for yourself? Over time, people have used a long list of names for the Indigenous Peoples of the Americas, but those words have rarely been what they would call themselves.

The power and meaning of labels comes not only from the choice of words but also from how those words are said. Niin, an Anishinaabe woman of both Cree and Ojibway descent, talked in an interview about the first time in her childhood when someone called her an "Indian."

> I'm not sure whether I was in grade one or in grade two; actually I think it was in kindergarten, because my Mom was home at that time. I remember being outside for recess. You know, everyone was running around, playing in the middle of the field. All of a sudden I stopped because I realized that a few of the kids who were in my classroom had formed a circle around me. They were going around and around the circle and I realized I was in the middle of this circle. I was trying to figure out what the heck is going on here? They were saying something and I started listening to them. They were saying "Indian, Indian, Indian." And I was like what? I really didn't understand myself, first and foremost, as an "Indian." Right in the middle of when they were doing that, the bell rang and everybody just turned toward the door and started walking in. I remember looking down on the ground wondering, what are they talking about Indian, Indian, Indian? I don't even know how that circle formed in the first place. I didn't catch it. It just seemed all of a sudden they were all around me and I just stopped, looking at them all. The bell rang right away. I just remember putting my head down, walking, looking at the grass, I was really thinking about, what was that all about? I didn't even remember it by the time we got to the door. Except for when I got home I asked my Mom.
>
> I remember when I went home, my mother was standing at the counter. She was baking something or other but she was working at the counter and I just walked up to her and I was watching what she was doing. I remember my chin barely touched the counter and I was watching her. I said, "Mom, what am I?" And she looked down at me and said really fast, "Were people asking you what you were?" I said, "Yes, they were calling me Indian." She said, "Tell them you're Canadian." I couldn't really figure out why she was sounding so stern and kind of angry. I just thought okay and I turned around but I remember that afternoon really clearly. I think why it stuck in my mind so much is because they were in a circle ridiculing me. And I don't even know. I didn't even take offence because I didn't know what they were doing. Even though they were calling me Indian, I was still going yeah, so what? So it always puzzled me about why, why they were calling me Indian. And because I didn't really feel any different from them, even though I knew my skin was darker, my hair was brown, and I had a shinier face. I really didn't feel any different from them or feel I was different from them.

> I just felt we were all just kids. I think that's when I started learning that there were different kinds of people. I knew that there were different kinds of people by just looking and seeing like different looking people but not people who are different from one another.[1]

CONNECTION QUESTIONS

1. What do you think the word *Indian* meant to the kids in Niin's class? What factors might have shaped her classmates' understanding of the word?

2. Why do you think Niin's mother told Niin she was Canadian? What did she want Niin to understand about herself?

3. Considering the rest of the story, what might Niin's mother have wanted Niin's classmates to learn?

4. Do you have a memory of becoming aware of differences? If so, what was it?

[1] Mary Young, *Pimatisiwin: Walking in a Good Way, a Narrative Inquiry into Language as Identity* (Manitoba: The Prolific Group, 2005), 47–48. Reproduced by permission from Pemmican Publishers.

READING

FINDING CONFIDENCE

In the following passage, Cameron Tuttle explains how her need for acceptance shaped her experience when she was in high school and came to understand that she was gay.

> No one bullied me in high school because absolutely no one knew I was gay. Definitely not me. It took me years to figure that out.
>
> I was one of those squeaky-clean, annoyingly mainstream, overachiever types. I got good grades, did student government, sang in musicals, played team sports, and joined lots of clubs to fatten up my college applications. But even though I was popular and friends with lots of different people, I felt alone, really alone, like no one knew the real me.
>
> How could they? I was trying so hard to be perfect.
>
> On the outside, I was a thriving, active, make-my-family-proud, successful teenager. But on the inside, I was emotionally numb, comatose, flat-lining. My mom had died of breast cancer two weeks before the beginning of ninth grade. She was an amazing mom, loving and supportive, and she gave me enough freedom to explore who I was so I could succeed or fail with my own personal style. After she died, I was devastated. But I was determined to prove to the world and to myself that I was okay.
>
> I found myself working really, really hard to be the best because I was scared. Scared of being different. Scared of being defective. Scared of feeling my feelings. So for years, I didn't let myself feel.
>
> I got a lot done in high school but I didn't have a lot of fun. And even though I wasn't ever bullied by other people, I was relentlessly bullied by my own thoughts and fears about who I was, how I was supposed to behave, and what would happen if I didn't.
>
> I actually had this pathetic idea that I would somehow let down my community—people I barely knew in the conservative, snooty neighborhood where I grew up—if I ended up being a lesbian. How ridiculous is that?
>
> Bullying isn't just what real people in real time say to you or try to do to you. Bullying is everywhere—it's in the words of fearful, judgmental parents who are trying to control you. (BTW: it's also in the words of well-meaning but misguided parents who are trying "to protect you from being hurt.") Bullying is in the news and in government policy. It's in the imagery of pop culture. It's in religion. And as a result, it gets into your head.
>
> How did it get better for me? Slowly. It helped that I went to college across the country, as far away as I possibly could go from my hometown without needing a passport.

I eventually found the guts to stand up to my inner bully, the judgmental, fearful, bossy voice in my head that kept telling me, You can't . . . You shouldn't . . . Don't you dare! And then I finally found the confidence to listen to my body and to my heart and to be honest with myself.

And then I moved to New York.

When I was living there, I met tons of people who were a lot like me—squeaky-clean, annoyingly mainstream overachievers who just happened to be gay: former high-school cheerleaders, homecoming kings, class officers, student leaders, star athletes. And I realized . . . yeah, I can do this. Yeah, I can be this. And now, I love being different—in my squeaky-clean, annoyingly mainstream way.[1]

CONNECTION QUESTIONS

1. How do you define "bullying"? How does Cameron Tuttle's story add to your thinking?

2. Create an identity chart for Tuttle. How might the identity chart you made for her be different from the one she would make for herself? What might be some differences between the way others see her and the way she sees herself?

3. What did it mean for Tuttle to find her own voice?

[1] Cameron Tuttle, "Too Good to Be True," in *It Gets Better: Coming Out, Overcoming Bullying, and Creating a Life Worth Living*, ed. Dan Savage and Terry Miller (New York: Plume, 2012), 130–32. Reproduced by permission from Cameron Tuttle.

READING

FINDING ONE'S VOICE

How much of our identities can we define for ourselves, and how much is determined by other influences, such as our families, our culture, and the circumstances of our lives? Writer Julius Lester defied other people's expectations on his journey toward understanding and defining his identity. Here, he reflects on the way violence and humiliation affected his childhood:

> I grew up in the forties and fifties in Kansas City, Kansas, and Nashville, Tennessee, with summers spent in Arkansas. The forties and fifties were not pleasant times for blacks and I am offended by white people who get nostalgic for the fifties. I have no nostalgia for segregation, for the "No Colored Allowed" signs covering the landscape like litter on the smooth, green grass of a park, I have no nostalgia for a time when I endangered my life if, while downtown shopping with my parents, I raised my eyes and accidentally met the eyes of a white woman. Black men and boys were lynched for this during my childhood and adolescence.[1]

Lester describes the way he survived those years as follows:

> I grew up in a violent world. Segregation was a deathly spiritual violence, not only in its many restrictions on where we could live, eat, go to school, and go after dark. There was also the constant threat of physical death if you looked at a white man in what he considered the wrong way or if he didn't like your attitude. There was also the physical violence of my community . . . What I have realized is that on those nights I lay in bed reading westerns and detective novels, I was attempting to neutralize and withstand the violence that was so much a part of my dailiness. In westerns and mysteries I found a kind of mirror in which one element of my world—violence—was isolated and made less harmful to me.[2]

Not surprisingly, Lester found his voice in a book. He explains:

> One of the pivotal experiences of my life came when I was eighteen. I wandered into a bookstore in downtown Nashville one frosted, gray day in late autumn aware that I was looking for something: I was looking for myself, and I generally find myself while wandering through a bookstore, looking at books until I find the one that is calling me. On this particular day I wandered for quite a while until I picked up a paperback with the word *Haiku* on the cover. What is that? I wondered. I opened the book and read,
>
> > On a withered branch
> >
> > a crow has settled —
> >
> > autumn nightfall.
>
> I trembled and turned the pages hastily until my eyes stopped on these words:

A giant firefly;
that way, this way, that way, this —
and it passes by.

I read more of the brief poems, these voices from seventeenth-century Japan, and I knew: This is my voice. This simplicity, this directness, this way of using words to direct the soul to silence and beyond. This is my voice! I exulted inside. Then I stopped. How could I, a little colored kid from Nashville, Tennessee—and that is all I knew myself to be in those days like perpetual death knells—how could I be feeling that something written in seventeenth-century Japan could be my voice?

I almost put the book back, but that inner prompting which had led me to it would not allow such an act of self-betrayal. I bought the book and began writing haiku, and the study of haiku led to the study of Zen Buddhism, which led to the study of flower arranging, and I suspect I am still following the path that opened to me on that day when I was eighteen, though I no longer write haiku . . . [3]

I eventually understood that it made perfect sense for a little colored kid from Nashville, Tennessee, to recognize his voice in seventeenth-century Japanese poetry. Who we are by the sociological and political definitions of society has little to do with who we are.

In the quiet and stillness that surrounds us when we read a book, we are known to ourselves in ways we are not when we are with people. We enter a relationship of intimacy with the writer, and if the writer has written truly and if we give ourselves over to what is written, we are given the gift of ourselves in ways that surprise and catch the soul off guard.[4]

CONNECTION QUESTIONS

1. What barriers did society place in the way of Julius Lester's becoming the kind of person he wanted to be? How did he overcome these barriers?

2. When Lester found a book of haiku in the bookstore, why did he almost put it back?

3. Lester writes that when he found the book of haiku, "I knew: This is my voice." Have you ever found your voice in a work of art, music, literature, or film?

[1] Julius Lester, *Falling Pieces of the Broken Sky* (New York: Arcade, 1990), 69. Reproduced by permission of Menza-Barron Literary Agency.

[2] Lester, *Falling Pieces of the Broken Sky*, 71–73.

[3] Lester, *Falling Pieces of the Broken Sky*, 71–73.

[4] Lester, *Falling Pieces of the Broken Sky*, 71–73.

READING

GENDER AND IDENTITY

Sometimes our assumptions and expectations about others prevent us from seeing who they really are as individuals. Some of the most powerful expectations about people that we learn from our culture are about gender. A person's sex often leads us to make assumptions about that person's identity. Martha Minow, a legal scholar, explains:

> Of course, there are "real differences" in the world; each person differs in countless ways from each other person. But when we simplify and sort, we focus on some traits rather than others, and we assign consequences to the presence and absence of the traits we make significant. We ask, "What's the new baby?"—and we expect as an answer, boy or girl. That answer, for most of history, has spelled consequences for the roles and opportunities available to that individual.[1]

American author Lori Duron and her husband, Matt, have two children, both boys. She writes about what happened the first time her younger son, C.J., got a Barbie doll.

> For days after C.J. discovered her, Barbie never left his side. When I'd do a final bed check at night before I retired for the evening to watch reality television and sneak chocolate when no one was looking, I'd see his full head of auburn hair sticking out above his covers. Next to him there would be a tiny tuft of blonde hair sticking out as well.
>
> The next time we were at Target near the toy aisle—which I've always tried to pass at warp speed so the kids don't notice and beg me to buy them something—C.J. wanted to see "Barbie stuff." I led him to the appropriate aisle and he stood there transfixed, not touching a thing, just taking it all in. He was so overwhelmed that he didn't ask to buy a single thing. He finally walked away from the aisle speechless, as if he had just seen something so magical and majestic that he needed time to process it.
>
> He had, that day, discovered the pink aisles of the toy department. We had never been down those aisles; we had only frequented the blue aisles, when we ventured down the toy aisles at all. As far as C.J. was concerned, I had been hiding half the world from him.
>
> I felt bad about that, like I had deprived him because of my assumptions and expectations that he was a boy and boys liked boy things. Matt and I noticed that C.J. didn't really like any of the toys we provided for him, which were all handed down from his brother. We noticed that C.J. didn't go through the normal boy toy addictions that Chase [C.J.'s older brother] had gone through: he couldn't care less about balls, cars, dinosaurs, superheroes, The Wiggles, Bob the Builder, or Thomas the Tank Engine. What did he like to play with? We didn't worry ourselves much about finding the answer (a case of the second-born child not getting fussed over quite like the first-born); we trusted that in time something would draw him in. Which it did. It just wasn't at all what we were expecting.

> At about the eighteen- to twenty-four-month mark of a child's life, the gender-neutral toys disappear and toys that are marketed specifically to boys or to girls take over. We didn't realize it until later, but that divide in the toy world and our house being filled with only boy toys left C.J. a little lost at playtime. We and the rest of society had been pushing masculine stuff on him and enforcing traditional gender norms, when all he wanted was to brush long blonde hair and dress, undress, and re-dress Barbie . . . [2]

Reflecting on C.J.'s identity, Duron concludes:

> On the gender-variation spectrum of super-macho-masculine on the left all the way to super-girly-feminine on the right, C.J. slides fluidly in the middle; he's neither all pink nor all blue. He's a muddled mess or a rainbow creation, depending on how you look at it. Matt and I have decided to see the rainbow, not the muddle. But we didn't always see it that way.
>
> Initially, the sight of our son playing with girl toys or wearing girl clothes made our chests tighten, forged a lump in our throats, and, at times, made us want to hide him. There was anger, anxiety, and fear. We've evolved as parents as our younger son has evolved into a fascinating, vibrant person who is creative with gender. Sometimes, when I think of how we behaved as parents in C.J.'s gender nonconformity, I'm ashamed and embarrassed.[3]

CONNECTION QUESTIONS

1. What are the differences between the toys in the pink aisle and the toys in the blue aisle? What assumptions do the toys in these aisles reflect about what it means to be a boy or a girl?

2. How do you explain the anxiety, anger, and fear that Duron felt when C.J. started playing with the "girl toys"? How did her feelings change?

3. What are some other stereotypes about gender in your world? How do you respond to the assumptions people make about you because of your gender? To what extent do you accept or reject those assumptions?

[1] Martha Minow, *Making All the Difference: Inclusion, Exclusion, and American Law* (Ithaca, NY: Cornell University Press, 1990), 3.

[2] Lori Duron, *Raising My Rainbow: Adventures in Raising a Fabulous, Gender Creative Son* (New York: Broadway Books, 2013), 9–10. Reproduced by permission of Penguin Random House.

[3] Duron, *Raising My Rainbow*, 4.

READING

THE DANGER OF A SINGLE STORY

Chimamanda Ngozi Adichie is a writer who has won several awards for her novels, short stories, and essays. She was born in Nigeria, and she attended universities in both Nigeria and the United States. She continues to live in both countries. In her TED Talk "The Danger of a Single Story," Adichie describes the effects that labels can have on how we think about ourselves and others.

> I come from a conventional, middle-class Nigerian family. My father was a professor. My mother was an administrator. And so we had, as was the norm, live-in domestic help, who would often come from nearby rural villages. So, the year I turned eight, we got a new house boy. His name was Fide. The only thing my mother told us about him was that his family was very poor. My mother sent yams and rice, and our old clothes, to his family. And when I didn't finish my dinner, my mother would say, "Finish your food! Don't you know? People like Fide's family have nothing." So I felt enormous pity for Fide's family.
>
> Then one Saturday, we went to his village to visit, and his mother showed us a beautifully patterned basket made of dyed raffia that his brother had made. I was startled. It had not occurred to me that anybody in his family could actually make something. All I had heard about them was how poor they were, so that it had become impossible for me to see them as anything else but poor. Their poverty was my single story of them.
>
> Years later, I thought about this when I left Nigeria to go to university in the United States. I was 19. My American roommate was shocked by me. She asked where I had learned to speak English so well, and was confused when I said that Nigeria happened to have English as its official language. She asked if she could listen to what she called my "tribal music," and was consequently very disappointed when I produced my tape of Mariah Carey [an American pop singer]. She assumed that I did not know how to use a stove.
>
> What struck me was this: She had felt sorry for me even before she saw me. Her default position toward me, as an African, was a kind of patronizing, well-meaning pity. My roommate had a single story of Africa: a single story of catastrophe. In this single story, there was no possibility of Africans being similar to her in any way, no possibility of feelings more complex than pity, no possibility of a connection as human equals.
>
> I must say that before I went to the U.S., I didn't consciously identify as African. But in the U.S., whenever Africa came up, people turned to me. Never mind that I knew nothing about places like Namibia. But I did come to embrace this new identity, and in many ways I think of myself now as African . . .

So, after I had spent some years in the U.S. as an African, I began to understand my roommate's response to me. If I had not grown up in Nigeria, and if all I knew about Africa were from popular images, I too would think that Africa was a place of beautiful landscapes, beautiful animals, and incomprehensible people, fighting senseless wars, dying of poverty and AIDS, unable to speak for themselves and waiting to be saved by a kind, white foreigner. I would see Africans in the same way that I, as a child, had seen Fide's family . . .

And so, I began to realize that my American roommate must have throughout her life seen and heard different versions of this single story . . .

But I must quickly add that I too am just as guilty in the question of the single story. A few years ago, I visited Mexico from the U.S. The political climate in the U.S. at the time was tense, and there were debates going on about immigration. And, as often happens in America, immigration became synonymous with Mexicans. There were endless stories of Mexicans as people who were fleecing the healthcare system, sneaking across the border, being arrested at the border, that sort of thing.

I remember walking around on my first day in Guadalajara, watching the people going to work, rolling up tortillas in the marketplace, smoking, laughing. I remember first feeling slight surprise. And then, I was overwhelmed with shame. I realized that I had been so immersed in the media coverage of Mexicans that they had become one thing in my mind, the abject immigrant. I had bought into the single story of Mexicans and I could not have been more ashamed of myself. So that is how to create a single story, show a people as one thing, as only one thing, over and over again, and that is what they become.

It is impossible to talk about the single story without talking about power. There is a word, an Igbo [a language spoken in Nigeria] word, that I think about whenever I think about the power structures of the world, and it is "nkali." It's a noun that loosely translates to "to be greater than another." Like our economic and political worlds, stories too are defined by the principle of nkali: How they are told, who tells them, when they're told, how many stories are told, are really dependent on power.

Power is the ability not just to tell the story of another person, but to make it the definitive story of that person . . .

[T]he truth is that I had a very happy childhood, full of laughter and love, in a very close-knit family.

But I also had grandfathers who died in refugee camps. My cousin Polle died because he could not get adequate healthcare. One of my closest friends, Okoloma, died in a plane crash because our fire trucks did not have water. I grew up under repressive military governments that devalued education, so that sometimes, my parents were not paid their salaries. And so, as a child, I saw jam disappear from the breakfast table, then margarine disappeared, then bread became too expensive, then milk became rationed. And most of all, a kind of normalized political fear invaded our lives.

All of these stories make me who I am. But to insist on only these negative stories is to flatten my experience and to overlook the many other stories that formed me. The single story creates stereotypes, and the problem with stereotypes is not that they are untrue, but that they are incomplete. They make one story become the only story.

Of course, Africa is a continent full of catastrophes: There are immense ones, such as the horrific rapes in Congo, and depressing ones, such as the fact that 5,000 people apply for one job vacancy in Nigeria. But there are other stories that are not about catastrophe, and it is very important, it is just as important, to talk about them.

I've always felt that it is impossible to engage properly with a place or a person without engaging with all of the stories of that place and that person. The consequence of the single story is this: It robs people of dignity. It makes our recognition of our equal humanity difficult. It emphasizes how we are different rather than how we are similar.

So what if before my Mexican trip, I had followed the immigration debate from both sides, the U.S. and the Mexican? What if my mother had told us that Fide's family was poor and hardworking? What if we had an African television network that broadcast diverse African stories all over the world? . . .

. . . What if my roommate knew about the female lawyer who recently went to court in Nigeria to challenge a ridiculous law that required women to get their husband's consent before renewing their passports? What if my roommate knew about Nollywood, full of innovative people making films despite great technical odds, films so popular that they really are the best example of Nigerians consuming what they produce? What if my roommate knew about my wonderfully ambitious hair braider, who has just started her own business selling hair extensions? Or about the millions of other Nigerians who start businesses and sometimes fail, but continue to nurse ambition?

Every time I am home I am confronted with the usual sources of irritation for most Nigerians: our failed infrastructure, our failed government, but also by the incredible resilience of people who thrive despite the government, rather than because of it. I teach writing workshops in Lagos every summer, and it is amazing to me how many people apply, how many people are eager to write, to tell stories . . .

Stories matter. Many stories matter. Stories have been used to dispossess and to malign, but stories can also be used to empower and to humanize. Stories can break the dignity of a people, but stories can also repair that broken dignity.

The American writer Alice Walker wrote this about her Southern relatives who had moved to the North. She introduced them to a book about the Southern life that they had left behind. "They sat around, reading the book themselves, listening to me read the book, and a kind of paradise was regained." I would like to end with this thought: That when we reject the single story, when we realize that there is never a single story about any place, we regain a kind of paradise.

[1] Chimamanda Adichie, "The Danger of a Single Story," TED video (filmed July 2009, posted October 2009), 18:49, accessed March 28, 2016, https://www.ted.com/talks/chimamanda_adichie_the_danger_of_a_single_story.

HANDOUT

THE DANGER OF A SINGLE STORY

VIEWING/READING GUIDE

DIRECTIONS: As you watch the video or read aloud the text with your class, respond to the following questions.

1. How does Adichie describe herself at the beginning of her talk? What words and phrases might she put on her own identity chart?

2. Later in the story, we learn how other people view her. How do those views differ from how she describes herself?

3. According to Adichie, what dilemmas can arise when others view us differently than we view ourselves?

READING

UNIVERSE OF OBLIGATION

What does it mean to be a member of a group? In groups we meet our most basic needs; in groups we learn a language and a culture or way of life. In groups we also satisfy our yearning to belong, receive comfort in times of trouble, and find companions who share our dreams, values, and beliefs. Groups also provide security and protection from those who might wish to do us harm. Therefore, how a group defines its membership matters. Belonging can have significant advantages; being excluded can leave a person vulnerable.

How the members of a group, a nation, or a community define who belongs and who does not has a lot to do with how they define their universe of obligation. Sociologist Helen Fein coined this phrase to describe the group of individuals within a society "toward whom obligations are owed, to whom rules apply, and whose injuries call for amends."[1] In other words, a society's universe of obligation includes those people who that society believes deserve respect and whose rights it believes are worthy of protection.

A society's universe of obligation can change. Individuals and groups that are respected and protected members of a society at one time may find themselves outside of the universe of obligation when circumstances are different—such as during a war or economic depression. Beliefs and attitudes that are widely shared among members of a society may also affect the way that society defines its universe of obligation. For instance, throughout history, beliefs and attitudes about religion, gender, and race have helped to determine which people a society protects and which people it does not.

Although Fein uses the term to describe the way nations determine membership, we might also refer to an individual's universe of obligation to describe the circle of other individuals that person feels a responsibility to care for and protect. Rabbi Jonathan Sacks describes how individuals often define those for whom they feel responsible: "[Eighteenth-century philosopher] David Hume noted that our sense of empathy diminishes as we move outward from the members of our family to our neighbors, our society, and the world. Traditionally, our sense of involvement with the fate of others has been in inverse proportion to the distance separating us and them."[2]

Scholar and social activist Chuck Collins defines his universe of obligation differently from the example Sacks offers. In the 1980s, Collins gave the half-million dollars that he inherited from his family to charity. Collins told journalist Ian Parker:

> Of course, we have to respond to our immediate family, but, once they're O.K., we need to expand the circle. A larger sense of family is a radical idea, but we get into trouble as a society when we don't see that we're in the same boat.[3]

CONNECTION QUESTIONS

1. What factors influence the way a society defines its universe of obligation? In what ways might a nation or community signal who is part of its universe of obligation and who is not?

2. What do you think might be some of the consequences for those who are not within a society's universe of obligation?

3. What factors influence how an individual defines his or her universe of obligation? In what ways might an individual show others who is part of his or her universe of obligation and who is not?

4. In the 1800s, sociologist William Graham Sumner wrote, "Every man and woman in society has one big duty. That is, to take care of his or her own self." Do you agree with Sumner? Why or why not? Is it wrong to prioritize caring for those closest to you over others? How does Sumner's suggestion about how we define our universe of obligation differ from Chuck Collins's view?

5. How would you describe your nation's universe of obligation? Your school's? Your own?

[1] Helen Fein, *Accounting for Genocide* (New York: Free Press, 1979), 4.

[2] Jonathan Sacks, *The Dignity of Difference: How to Avoid the Clash of Civilizations* (London: Continuum, 2002), 30.

[3] Ian Parker, "The Gift," *New Yorker*, August 2, 2004, 60.

HANDOUT

OVERVIEW OF ANTI-JUDAISM AND ANTISEMITISM

DIRECTIONS: As you are reading, annotate the text by completing the following steps:

1. Circle words that are unfamiliar.
2. Put a question mark (?) in the margin in places where you feel confused.
3. Stop and answer the questions in the boxes. Underline the place(s) in the text where you found the answer to a question.

Judaism is the oldest monotheistic religion. Throughout much of the faith's history, Jews lived in territories ruled by other groups. They were often treated as outsiders and blamed for disasters suffered by the societies in which they lived. Continuous rumors, lies, myths, and misinformation about Jews have existed throughout history. Many of them persist in the contemporary world. Often this hatred has led to violence.

In 63 BCE, the Romans conquered Jerusalem, the center of Jewish life. They incorporated ancient Israel, the land where the Jews lived, into the Roman Empire. The Romans were brutal rulers who demanded that those they ruled worship their numerous gods. Jews worshipped only one god. The Romans responded with persecution and violence. They destroyed the center of Jewish life, the temple in Jerusalem, in 70 CE. In 130 CE, the Romans attacked Jerusalem again. They displaced much of the Jewish population from the region that the Jews considered their homeland.

Why did the Romans view the Jews as a threat?

thought diffently

During this period of Roman rule, a new faith, Christianity, emerged from Judaism. Jesus and his early followers were Jews. But as Christianity spread after the Romans executed Jesus, early Christians distanced themselves from Jews. This was partly to avoid being persecuted by the Romans. Christianity and Judaism eventually became separate and competing religions. By the 300s, Christianity became the official religion of the Roman Empire. Jews remained a minority.

Over time, lies and myths developed about Jews. Christian Roman society increasingly portrayed them as "Other." They were also blamed for various social ills. Among these myths was the false charge that Jews, not Romans, were responsible for the death of Christ. Another powerful lie charged Jews with associating with the devil.

Throughout the Middle Ages, European Christian armies attacked Jewish communities. Jews were also falsely blamed for causing the Black Death. They were forced in some places in Europe to live in ghettos and wear identifying badges. In other places, they were driven away entirely. This happened in 1492. King Ferdinand and Queen Isabella forced Jews to leave the Iberian Peninsula unless they converted. But in the 1500s, not even conversion was enough to save Jews in Spain. The claim emerged among many Christians that those born as Jews had "Jewish blood." This claim stated that conversion to Christianity did not change Jews' fundamental identity.

For what events did Christians blame Jews during the Middle Ages? What were the consequences for many Jewish communities? Killing Jesus, Disease, Devil

Later in the 1500s, Christians known as Protestants broke away from the Church of Rome. Many Protestants thought that Jews would convert to their new Christian faith. When that did not happen, Protestant leader Martin Luther turned on Jews. He called for synagogues and Jewish homes to be set on fire.

The ideas of the Enlightenment had spread across Europe by the 1700s. Among those ideas was that society could be improved through the use of human reason and science and through the ideals of equality. Between the late 1700s and early 1900s, laws and restrictions that discriminated against Jews were lifted in many European societies. In many places, Jews were allowed to participate more fully in the politics, economy, and social life of the places they lived.

As restrictions on Jews loosened across Europe in the 1800s, Jews became more integrated into European society. Some Jews became successful and visible leaders in a variety of professions, and a few became high-ranking government officials. This sparked a backlash from those who continued to be prejudiced against Jews or felt threatened by their increasing success (even though most European Jews remained poor). False conspiracy theories spread across Europe that Jews secretly controlled powerful governments. The theories also stated that Jews controlled financial institutions and sought to enrich themselves at the expense of non-Jewish Europeans.

How did the Enlightenment ideas impact the treatment of Jews in Europe?

During the same period, the field of "race science" emerged in Europe and North America. This happened in part to portray slavery and other divisions in society as "natural."

Race scientists who divided humans into separate races began to count Jews as a race. In 1878, German Wilhelm Marr popularized the idea that Jews are a distinct and dangerous race. He called them the "Semitic" race. He believed that this race was assaulting Germany and decreasing the fortunes of true "Aryan" Germans. "Aryans" were a mythical, supposedly superior race. Many northern Europeans believed they had descended from the "Aryan" race. Marr coined the term "antisemitism" to describe his belief that Jews were dangerous and should not be allowed to participate in German society.

How did Wilhelm Marr apply ideas of "race" to Jews? How did "race science" support his views?

Antisemitism became common across Europe in the early 1900s. Jews were falsely blamed for the destruction and defeat suffered by Germany and its allies in World War I. They were also blamed for the communist revolution that overthrew the tsar in Russia. Thus, they inspired fear in capitalist societies across Europe. These myths and lies were used to justify increasing discrimination and violence against Jews in the twentieth century.

READING

"WE DON'T CONTROL AMERICA" AND OTHER MYTHS, PART 1

Miriam observes:

> Last year I tutored at this nursing school. This woman was from Guatemala. I'm sure she's educated, but she didn't speak English. My job was to teach her enough English so she could pass the test to get in. One day she said, "Miriam, are you Jewish?" I said, "Yeah." She said, "You know how I knew? Because you're very smart and you dress modestly." Then she said, "The Jews are the people of God—it says so in the Bible. That's why they're very smart and wealthy."
>
> I didn't know what to say. If you're Jewish, there is definitely an emphasis on being smart and succeeding in school. If people think that, then OK. But it's a problem to think that all Jews are wealthy when they're not. I was in Argentina last quarter. They have this huge economic crisis and a lot of extreme poverty. Synagogues are feeding lots and lots of hungry people who are Jews. No one can pay tuition anymore at the Jewish schools. Anti-Semitism is more of an issue there. A woman from Uruguay told a friend of mine that Jews run everything in Argentina.
>
> People's willingness to believe things like that is weird. That's where I think stereotypes become a problem. It's not OK to say, "All Jews are wealthier," or "The Jews run things," or "There's something about the Jews."[1]

[1] "There's Something About the Jews," in Pearl Gaskins, *I Believe In . . . : Christian, Jewish, and Muslim Young People Speak About Their Faith* (Chicago: Cricket Books, 2004), 92.

READING

"WE DON'T CONTROL AMERICA" AND OTHER MYTHS, PART 2

Darcy notes:

> Sometimes it's just innocent questions: people don't know better. A Jewish girlfriend of mine was asked if it's true that Jews freeze the placentas of their babies and then eat them. No. But there are definitely versions of the blood libel still around—[the lie] that Jews use the blood of Christian children to make their matzo for Passover. . . .
>
> I have a classmate who is Egyptian. She came with me to synagogue once and was looking through the prayer book, which is in Hebrew and English. She was looking for the part where it says we should kill all the Arabs, because that's what she was always taught. But there isn't anything in the prayer book or anything else about that because Jews don't believe that. We don't teach our children to hate Arabs or that they or any other non-Jews must die.
>
> She also thinks that Jews rule the U.S., which a lot of people think. We don't control America. In fact, until very recently, in many ways we were similar to blacks. It was fashionable to dislike Jews. We got blackballed from country clubs. If you look at charters for covenant-controlled communities, the old charters will actually list in their rules: "No blacks, no Jews. Mow your lawn once a week." They just put it in like it was a normal thing.[1]

[1] "There's Something About the Jews," in Pearl Gaskins, *I Believe In . . . : Christian, Jewish, and Muslim Young People Speak About Their Faith* (Chicago: Cricket Books, 2004), 92.

READING

"WE DON'T CONTROL AMERICA" AND OTHER MYTHS, PART 3

Olympic gymnast Kerri Strug writes:

> I have heard the same question over and over since I received my gold medal in gymnastics on the Olympic podium. "You're Jewish?" people ask in a surprised tone. Perhaps it is my appearance or the stereotype that Jews and sports don't mix that makes my Jewish heritage so unexpected. I think about the attributes that helped me reach that podium: perseverance when faced with pain, years of patience and hope in an uncertain future, and a belief and devotion to something greater than myself. It makes it hard for me to believe that I did not look Jewish up on the podium. In my mind, those are attributes that have defined Jews throughout history.[1]

[1] Kerri Strug, "You're Jewish?" in *I Am Jewish: Personal Reflections Inspired by the Last Words of Daniel Pearl*, ed. Judea and Ruth Pearl (Woodstock, VT: Jewish Lights, 2004), 98.

HANDOUT

INTRODUCTION TO THE WEIMAR REPUBLIC

DIRECTIONS: **Write a D next to information about the Weimar Republic that represents characteristics of a democracy and an X next to information that describes problems or challenges for a democracy.**

From Monarchy to Democracy

After World War I, Germany's political leaders sought to transform Germany from a monarchy to a democracy, called the Weimar Republic (1918–1933). The Weimar Constitution divided power into three branches of government. Elections were held for the president and the Reichstag (the legislature), while the judicial branch was appointed.

The Weimar Constitution

Adopted on August 11, 1919, the new Weimar Constitution spelled out the "basic rights and obligations" of government officials and the citizens they served. Most of those rights and obligations had not existed in Germany under the kaiser, including equality before the law, freedom of religion, and privacy. Despite the inclusion of these rights in the Weimar Constitution, individual freedom was not fully protected. Old laws that denied freedoms continued, including laws that discriminated against homosexual men and "Gypsies" (the name, considered derogatory today, used to describe two groups of people called the Sinti and Roma).

The Reichstag

Germans voted for a party, rather than a candidate, to fill the Reichstag (the German legislature). The elections determined the percentage of seats each party received in the Reichstag, but the parties themselves selected the individuals who filled each allotted seat. For example, if a party received 36% of the vote, they would get 36% of the seats in the Reichstag.

The Roles of President and Chancellor

As head of the government, the president controlled the nation's armed forces and had the power to dismiss the Reichstag, triggering new elections. The president also appointed the nation's chancellor. In a parliamentary system, the chancellor (or prime minister, in some countries) is in charge of the day-to-day operations of government. During the first ten years of the Weimar Republic, the president usually appointed a chancellor from the party that had the most seats in the Reichstag.

Forming a Majority

No single party ever held a majority in the Reichstag during the Weimar period. Thus, two or more parties often banded together to form a majority to run the legislature. But almost any disagreement between parties might break up such a coalition. When that occurred, a new election would be held, which happened 20 times during the Weimar period.

Article 48

Article 48 of the Weimar Constitution gave the president special emergency powers. If "public order and security are seriously disturbed or threatened," the president was empowered to suspend civil liberties and enact laws without the consent of the Reichstag.

Article 48 was intended to be a safety valve to protect Germany during state emergencies by enabling leaders to act quickly. But the president alone was to decide whether an emergency existed, and the first president of the Weimar Republic, Friedrich Ebert, invoked Article 48 to issue decrees 136 times, only occasionally in times of actual emergency.

Violence in the Weimar Government

Dozens of political parties competed for the support of German citizens. In some elections, ballots listed more than 30 parties to choose from. Many political parties had their own private armies, or paramilitaries. As a result, political disagreements and arguments on the streets often turned violent.

HANDOUT

WEIMAR REPUBLIC IMAGES

WEIMAR REPUBLIC IMAGE 1

WEIMAR REPUBLIC IMAGE 2

WEIMAR REPUBLIC IMAGE 3

WEIMAR REPUBLIC IMAGE 4

WEIMAR REPUBLIC IMAGE 5

WEIMAR REPUBLIC IMAGES KEY

1. *Metropolis* by Otto Dix (1928)

In addition to his depictions of World War I (*Wounded Soldier*), Otto Dix was known for his ruthless criticism of German society during the Weimar years.

Credit: akg-images

2. *The Agitator* by George Grosz (1928)

Grosz is one of the most important artists associated with the New Objectivity movement. New Objectivists believed that they were challenging the public to see the world as it really was, rather than as they would like it to be. Grosz's paintings and sketches often offered critical judgments of German society during the Weimar Republic.

Credit: Collection Stedelijk Museum Amsterdam

3. Marlene Dietrich in the film *Blue Angel* (1930)

Blue Angel, directed by Josef von Sternberg, was Germany's first full-length "talkie," a motion picture with sound as opposed to a silent film. The film follows the story of a college professor who is undone by his attraction to Lola-Lola, a cabaret dancer played by German American Marlene Dietrich. The film made Dietrich an international film star, and she continued her acting career in the United States.

Credit: MARKA / Alamy

4. *Kitchen Knife* by Hannah Höch (1919)

Höch's work consisted primarily of collages, often made from photographs. Höch was part of the Dada movement, which formed in part as a reaction to the death and destruction from World War I. Dada artists prized irrationality and considered their work "anti-art."

Credit: bpk, Berlin / Staatliche Museen / Jörg P. Anders / Art Resource, NY

5. *The Triadic Ballet* (1926)

The Triadic Ballet was created by Oskar Schlemmer, a painter, sculptor, designer, and choreographer who taught at the Bauhaus art school in Germany during the Weimar Republic. Schlemmer's ballet represented the Bauhaus style: uncluttered, modern, and geometric.

Credit: The J. Paul Getty Museum, Los Angeles

HANDOUT

EDUCATION IN THE WEIMAR REPUBLIC

DIRECTIONS: **As you are reading, annotate the text by completing the following steps:**

1. **Circle words that are unfamiliar.**
2. **Put a question mark (?) in the margin in places where you feel confused.**
3. **Answer the questions that follow the text.**

In the Weimar Republic, Germany's schools remained centers of tradition. Most teachers were conservative, both in their way of teaching and in their politics, and many were anti-socialist and antisemitic. A young man known as Klaus describes his schooling in the 1920s:

> We were taught history as a series of facts. We had to learn dates, names, places of battles. Periods during which Germany won wars were emphasized. Periods during which Germany lost wars were sloughed over. We heard very little about World War I, except that the Versailles peace treaty was a disgrace, which someday, in some vague way, would be rectified. In my school, one of the best in Berlin, there were three courses in Greek and Roman history, four in medieval history, and not one in government. If we tried to relate ideas we got from literature or history to current events, our teachers changed the subject.
>
> I really don't believe that anyone was deliberately trying to evade politics. Those teachers really seemed to think that what went on in the Greek and Roman Empires was more important than what was happening on the streets of Berlin and Munich. They considered any attempt to bring up current political questions a distraction . . . because we hadn't done our homework.
>
> And there was always a great deal of homework in a school like mine, which prepared students for the university. At the end of our senior year, we were expected to take a detailed and exceedingly tough exam called the Abitur. How we did on the exam could determine our whole future. Again, the Abitur concentrated on our knowledge of facts, not on interpretation or on the expression of personal ideas.[1]

[1] Ellen Switzer, *How Democracy Failed* (New York: Atheneum, 1977), 62–63. Reproduced by permission from Curtis Brown, Ltd.

1. Record the title, and write a brief summary (three or four sentences) of this reading.

2. What kind of education do you think would best prepare students to be citizens in a democracy? Do you think the education Klaus describes would prepare students for participation in a democracy? Explain your thinking.

HANDOUT

VOICES IN THE DARK

DIRECTIONS: As you are reading, annotate the text by completing the following steps:

1. Circle words that are unfamiliar.
2. Put a question mark (?) in the margin in places where you feel confused.
3. Answer the questions that follow the text.

Life in Weimar Germany was often unpredictable, as a former soldier, Henry Buxbaum, discovered one evening in the early 1920s:

> The train was pitch-dark. The lights were out, nothing uncommon after the war when the German railroads were in utter disrepair and very few things functioned orderly. . . . That night, we were seven or eight people in the dark, fourth-class compartment, sitting in utter silence till one of the men started the usual refrain: "Those God-damned Jews, they are at the root of all our troubles." Quickly, some of the others joined in. I couldn't see them and had no idea who they were, but from their voices they sounded like younger men. They sang the same litany over and over again, blaming the Jews for everything that has gone wrong with Germany and for anything else wrong in this world. It went on and on, a cacophony of obscenities, becoming more vicious and at the same time more unbearable with each new sentence echoing in my ears. Finally, I couldn't stand it any longer. I knew very well that to start up with them would get me into trouble, and that to answer them wasn't exactly the height of wisdom, but I couldn't help it. . . . I began naturally with the announcement: "Well, I am a Jew and etc., etc." That was the signal they needed. Now they really went after me, threatening me physically. I didn't hold my tongue as the argument went back and forth. They began jostling me till one of them . . . probably more encouraged by the darkness than by his own valor, suggested: "Let's throw the Jew out of the train." Now, I didn't dare ignore this signal, and from then on I kept quiet. I knew that silence for the moment was better than falling under the wheels of a moving train. One of the men in our compartment, more vicious in his attacks than the others, got off the train with me in Friedburg. When I saw him under the dim light of the platform, I recognized him as a fellow I knew well from our soccer club. . . . I would never have suspected this man of harboring such rabid, antisemitic feelings.[1]

Buxbaum's experience would not have been uncommon in Germany in the 1920s. Antisemitic conspiracy theories abounded in post-war Germany, permeating all the way to the highest levels of government. In 1919, Erich Ludendorff, one of Germany's top military leaders, falsely claimed that Jews were one of several groups responsible for the nation's defeat. As proof, he cited the *Protocols of the Elders of Zion*, a document supposedly containing the minutes of a secret meet-

[1] Henry Buxbaum, "Recollections," in *Jewish Life in Germany: Memoirs from Three Centuries*, ed. Monika Richarz, trans. Stella P. Rosenfeld and Sidney Rosenfeld (Bloomington: Indiana University Press, 1991), 303–04.

ing of Jewish leaders. At that supposed meeting, the "Elders" allegedly plotted to take over the world. In fact, the *Protocols of the Elders of Zion* is a forgery; Russian secret police wrote it in the early 1900s to incite hatred against Jews.

In the 1920s, Germany's 500,000 Jews accounted for less than 1% of the total population of about 61 million. Yet by focusing on Jews as "the enemy," antisemites made it seem as if Jews were everywhere and were responsible for everything that went wrong in the nation.

1. Record the title, and write a brief summary (three or four sentences) of this reading.

2. What role did the darkness play in the incident described in this reading? What role did the presence of a group of people who shared similar attitudes play?

3. What claims about Jews did the *Protocols of the Elders of Zion* make? What accounted for the popularity of the *Protocols* in Germany?

HANDOUT

HYPERINFLATION AND THE GREAT DEPRESSION

A woman takes a basket of banknotes to buy cabbage at a market during the 1923 hyperinflation in Weimar Germany.

Roger-Viollet / The Image Works

DIRECTIONS: As you are reading, annotate the text by completing the following steps:

1. Circle words that are unfamiliar.
2. Put a question mark (?) in the margin in places where you feel confused.
3. Answer the questions that follow the text.

Beginning in the fall of 1922, an extreme inflation, or hyperinflation, took hold of the German economy. During periods of inflation, prices rise continuously as the value of a currency drops sharply.

Many European countries experienced inflation after the war, but nowhere did prices rise as rapidly as they did in Germany. On some days, the value of the mark (the unit of German currency) fell almost hourly.

VALUE OF GERMAN CURRENCY

DATE	MARKS	US DOLLARS
1918	4.2	1
1921	75	1
1922	400	1
January 1923	7000	1
July 1923	160,000	1
August 1923	1,000,000	1
November 1, 1923	1,300,000,000	1
November 15, 1923	1,300,000,000,000	1
November 16, 1923	4,200,000,000,000	1

As a result of the inflation, Germans who had their savings in banks or were living on pensions or disability checks found themselves virtually bankrupt. Workers increasingly discovered that no matter how high their wages rose, they could not keep up with rapidly soaring prices.

Artist George Grosz described what shopping was like in those days:

> Lingering at the [shop] window was a luxury because shopping had to be done immediately. Even an additional minute meant an increase in price. One had to buy quickly because a rabbit, for example, might cost two million marks more by the time it took

> to walk into the store. A few million marks meant nothing, really. It was just that it meant more lugging. The packages of money needed to buy the smallest item had long since become too heavy for trouser pockets. They weighed many pounds . . . People had to start carting their money around in wagons and knapsacks. I used a knapsack.[1]

In October of 1929, a worldwide depression began, one that exacerbated the economic problems Germany had faced with hyperinflation. A depression is a severe economic downturn that forces businesses to decrease production and lay off workers. Germany felt the effects of the depression almost immediately. By 1932, 6 million Germans were unemployed in a nation of about 60 million people. Among them were Lea Langer Grundig, who was a Communist, and her husband, Hans. Like other job seekers, they stood in long lines at labor exchanges day after day:

> Unemployment became a tragedy for many. Not only because of the poverty that mutely sat at their table at all times. Not working, doing nothing, producing nothing—work that not only provided food, but also, despite all the harassment and drudgery, was satisfying, developed skills, and stimulated thinking; work, a human need—it was not available; and wherever it was lacking, decay, malaise, and despair set in . . .
>
> The grim poverty, the hopelessness, the laws governing the crisis that were incomprehensible for many, all these made people ripe for "miracles." Sects shot out of the ground. Diviners of the stars or coffee grounds, palm readers, graphologists, speculators and swindlers, clairvoyants and miracle workers had a great time; they reaped rich harvests among the poor, who along with their poverty and idleness fell prey to foolishness.[2]

[1] George Grosz, *A Little Yes and a Big No: The Autobiography of George Grosz*, trans. L. S. Dorin (New York: Dial, 1946), 63.

[2] From Lea Grundig, "Visions and History," in *The Nazi Germany Sourcebook: An Anthology of Texts*, ed. Roderick Stackelberg and Sally A. Winkle (London: Routledge, 2002), 97.

1. Record the title, and write a brief summary (three or four sentences) of this reading.

2. How did inflation change daily life in Germany?

3. How might a depression change attitudes about "we" and "they"? How might it affect a country's universe of obligation?

HANDOUT

WOMEN IN THE WEIMAR REPUBLIC

A crowd of women wait in line at a polling station in the Weimar Republic in 1919, the first year women were allowed to vote.

ullstein bild / Contributor / Getty Images

DIRECTIONS: As you are reading, annotate the text by completing the following steps:

1. Circle words that are unfamiliar.
2. Put a question mark (?) in the margin in places where you feel confused.
3. Answer the questions that follow the text.

At the turn of the twentieth century, women throughout Europe and North America were demanding that their governments give them the right to vote. Germany was no exception; women began to hold demonstrations for women's suffrage there as early as 1910. They succeeded in 1919, when Article 109 of the Weimar Constitution stated that men and women have the same fundamental rights and duties as citizens, including the right to vote and to hold office:

> Article 109: All Germans are equal in front of the law. In principle, men and women have the same rights and obligations.

During the years of the Weimar Republic, a majority of the electorate was female, in part because so many men had died in the war or were so physically or psychologically wounded that they were unlikely to vote. In 1919, the first year women could vote in Germany, they held 10% of the seats in the Reichstag, and their numbers continued to rise throughout the next decade.

During and after the war, the position of women in the workforce also began to change. While the proportion of women who had jobs remained about the same as before the war, women began to take new kinds of jobs that had previously been dominated by men. For instance, they began to fill more jobs that were visible throughout society, such as tram conductor and department store clerk, as well as (in smaller numbers) factory worker, lawyer, and doctor. While many of these positions would return to men after the war, women also moved into professions that many would continue to associate with women in the years that followed, such as teaching, social work, and secretarial work. All in all, more than 11 million women were employed in Germany in 1918, accounting for 36% of the workforce.[1]

[1] Detlev Peukert, *The Weimar Republic: The Crisis of Classical Modernity* (New York: Hill and Wang, 1992), 96–97; Richard J. Evans, *The Coming of the Third Reich* (New York: Penguin, 2003), 127.

1. Record the title, and write a brief summary (three or four sentences) of this reading.

2. Why do you think women won the right to vote in Germany in 1919? What is significant about that date?

3. What were some of the reasons women were more represented in the German government after World War I than they had been before the war?

4. How might the changes discussed in this reading have affected Germany's universe of obligation?

READING

NEGOTIATING PEACE

The Allied countries—including the United States, Britain, France, Italy, and Japan—negotiated the peace treaty at the Palace of Versailles in France from January 1919 to January 1920. The final Treaty of Versailles contained 440 articles, and Germans had no choice but to accept it.

Article 231 of the treaty explained who would pay for the enormous cost of the war and the damage in the war-torn Allied countries:

> Article 231
>
> The Allied and Associated Governments affirm and Germany accepts the responsibility of Germany and her allies for causing all the loss and damage to which the Allied and Associated Governments and their nationals have been subjected as a consequence of the war imposed upon them by the aggression of Germany and her allies.

Other portions of the treaty stated the following:

- Germany would limit the size of its military to fewer than 100,000 soldiers.
- Germany would have new borders in Europe, losing about 13% of its area.
- Germany would lose all colonies and other overseas territories.

Germans grew more angry when the terms of the Treaty of Versailles were made public in May 1919. Many Germans felt that their nation had been humiliated by the further loss of territory and military power imposed by the treaty.

HANDOUT

THE BUBBLING CAULDRON

Artist George Grosz said that the Weimar Republic was like a "bubbling cauldron." He wrote: "You could not see who was heating the cauldron; you could merely see it merrily bubbling, and you could feel that heat increasing."[1]

DIRECTIONS: **In this activity, you will use a graphic organizer based on Grosz's image to show your understanding of the Weimar Republic. Label the image of the cauldron as follows:**

- **Who or what added fuel to the fire?** Outside of the cauldron, write the names of people, groups, events, and circumstances that caused tension and conflict in German society during the Weimar Republic (e.g., paramilitary groups).

- **What was the fuel for the fire?** In each log beneath the cauldron, write words and phrases describing human behaviors, feelings, and emotions in German society during the Weimar Republic (e.g., violence). Draw additional logs if you need them.

- **What was in the cauldron?** In the cauldron, write the aspects of German society that were affected by the behaviors and feelings you labeled in the logs (e.g., freedom of speech).

For instance, you might say that "paramilitary groups" added the "violence" log beneath the fire that created enough heat to affect the "freedom of speech" ingredient in the cauldron.

You can use words and phrases from the bank below as you label the image. You do not have to use all of the words provided. You may also add words and phrases that you think of on your own.

When you are finished, write your answers to the questions on the last page.

Anger	Values	Artists	Women's Rights
Humiliation	Hatred	Teachers	Frequent Elections
Alienation	Antisemitism	Paramilitary Groups	Article 48
Anxiety	World War I	Political Parties	Trust in Democracy
Fear	Treaty of Versailles	Voting	Germany's Universe of Obligation
Creativity	Hyperinflation	Intimidation	Trust in Neighbors
Violence	Great Depression	Weimar Constitution	
Uncertainty	Unemployment	Civil Rights	
Education	Leaders	Freedom of Speech	

[1] George Grosz, *An Autobiography*, trans. Nora Hodges (Berkeley: University of California Press, 1998), 149–50.

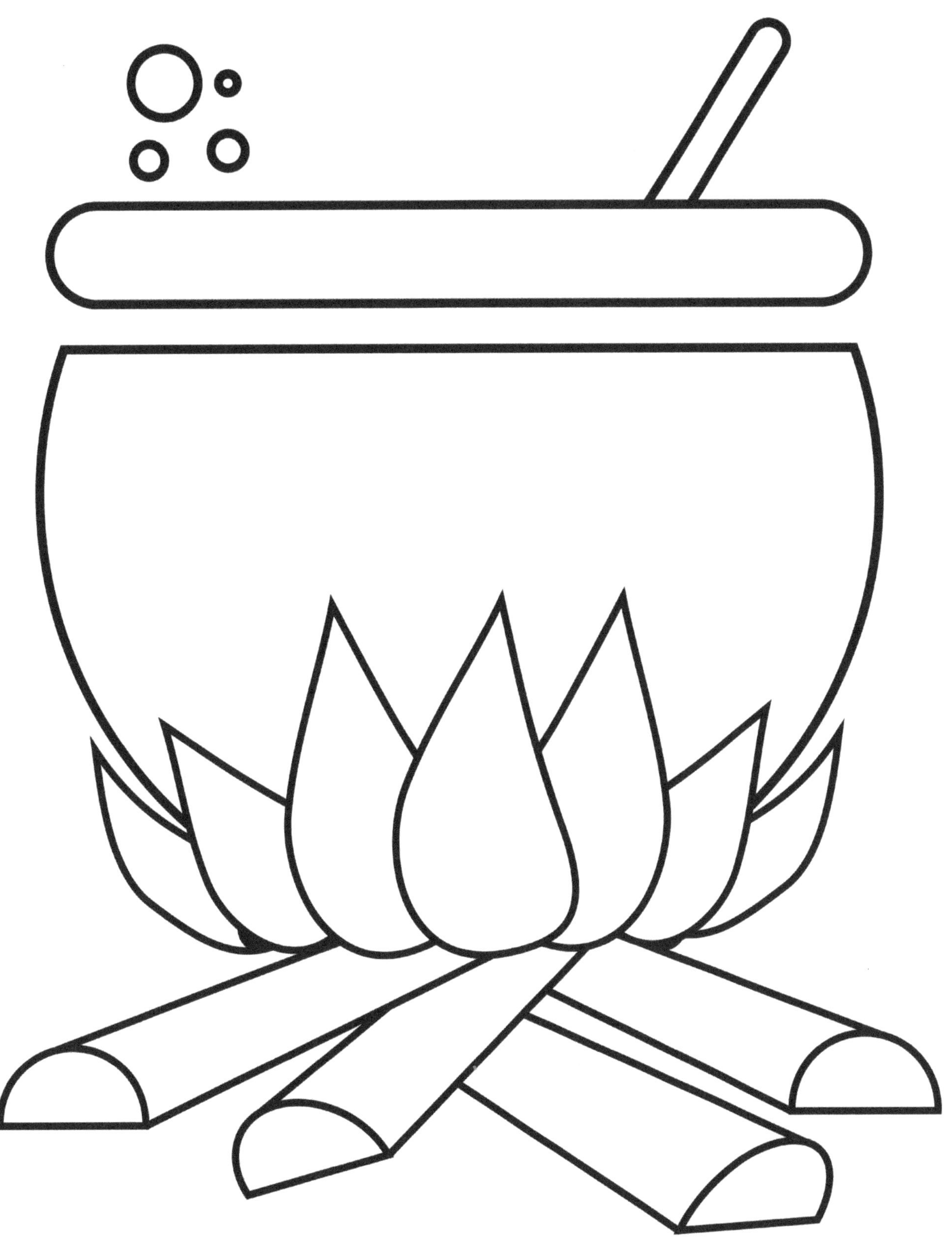

1. What do you think Grosz's metaphor means? What does it suggest about what it felt like to live in Germany during that time? What might be the result of the increasing "heat"?

2. What was the process like of labeling the cauldron graphic? What challenges did you encounter? What new conclusions did you draw about the Weimar Republic from this activity?

HANDOUT

HITLER'S RISE TO POWER, 1918–1933 VIEWING GUIDE

DIRECTIONS: As you view the film *Hitler's Rise to Power, 1918–1933*, record notes that help you answer the questions on this handout. Watch for moments where choices made by people other than Hitler contributed to Hitler's and the Nazi Party's eventual rise to power. Put a star by these notes.

1. How did German soldiers who returned from World War I affect the way German politics was conducted?

2. How did the National Socialist German Workers' Party (the Nazi Party) explain Germany's loss in World War I to the public? Who did the party blame for the loss?

3. While in prison for his failed attempt at staging a coup in Munich, Hitler wrote *Mein Kampf* (My Struggle), a book in which he shares his idea for how to take control of a people. What is his main idea?

4. What was the Nazis' primary campaign message in the early 1930s? How was it different from what we now know were the Nazis' two primary goals for Germany?

Respond to the following question after viewing the film:

5. What choices did you learn about in this video, made by people other than Hitler, that contributed to the possibility that Hitler and the Nazi Party could eventually rise to power in Germany?

READING

NATIONAL SOCIALIST GERMAN WORKERS' PARTY PLATFORM

The following list contains some of the provisions that Hitler proposed at the National Socialist German Workers' Party's first large party gathering in February 1920.

- We demand the unification of all Germans in a Greater Germany on the basis of the right of national self-determination.
- We demand . . . the revocation of the peace treaty of Versailles . . .
- We demand land and territory (colonies) to feed our people and to settle our surplus population.
- . . . Only those of German blood, whatever their creed, may be members of the nation. Accordingly, no Jew may be a member of the nation.
- Non-citizens may only live in Germany as guests and must be subject to laws for aliens.
- The right to vote . . . shall be enjoyed by the citizens . . . alone. We demand therefore that all official appointments, of whatever kind, whether in the Reich, in the states or in the smaller localities, shall be held by none but citizens.
- We demand that the State shall make its primary duty to provide a livelihood for its citizens. If it should prove impossible to feed the entire population, foreign nationals (non-citizens) must be deported . . .
- All non-German immigration must be prevented. We demand that all non-Germans who entered Germany after 2 November 1914 shall be required to leave immediately . . .
- . . . To facilitate the creation of a German national press we demand:
    - That all editors of, and contributors to newspapers appearing in the German language must be members of the nation;
    - That no non-German newspapers may appear without express permission of the State. They must not be printed in the German language;
    - That non-Germans shall be prohibited by law from participating financially in or influencing German newspapers . . .

The Party . . . is convinced that our nation can achieve permanent health only from within on the basis of the principle: The common interest before self-interest . . .

READING

HITLER IN POWER

In April 1932, Paul von Hindenburg, at the age of 84, remained president by defeating Hitler and his other challengers. He began his new term in office that spring by naming a new chancellor—Franz von Papen, a close friend and member of the Center Party. Papen ran the country for the rest of the year. When he failed to end the depression, another of Hindenburg's friends, General Kurt von Schleicher, who belonged to no party, took over in December. He was also unable to bring about a recovery and was forced to resign.

Hindenburg and his advisors were all conservatives who represented wealthy landowners, industrialists, and other powerful people. As the depression persisted, their popular support was shrinking. So in January of 1933, they decided to make a deal with Hitler. He had the popularity they lacked, and they had the power he needed. They also agreed on a number of points, including a fierce opposition to communism, hostility to democracy, and eagerness for *Lebensraum*—additional land for the German *Volk*.

Hindenburg's advisors believed that the responsibility of being in power would make Hitler moderate his views. They convinced themselves that they were wise enough and powerful enough to "control" Hitler. Also, they were certain that he, too, would fail to end the depression. And when he failed, they would step in to save the nation. Hitler fooled them all.

On January 30, 1933, Hitler was sworn in as chancellor of Germany. Because the Nazi Party did not control a majority of the Reichstag, they joined with the German National People's Party to form a coalition government—that is, one run by multiple political parties, usually with different but overlapping agendas. Nevertheless, Hitler accepted the appointment as if he had been named emperor of Germany and ignored the wishes of the other party. He and his fellow Nazis boasted that they would soon restore the nation and the "Aryan race" to greatness by ending so-called "Jewish racial domination" and eliminating the Communist threat. The result would be a "third Reich" (*Reich* is the German word for "empire"). The Nazis considered the Holy Roman Empire (952–1806) the "first Reich" and the empire established after the unification of the German states in 1871 the "second." Hitler was confident that his Third Reich would be the greatest of all, and it would last a thousand years.

HANDOUT

HITLER'S RISE TO POWER, 1933–1934 VIEWING GUIDE

While viewing the film, take notes in response to the first two questions listed below.

1. Why was Hitler vulnerable when he was appointed chancellor?

2. How did Hitler solidify his hold on power in 1933 and 1934? List as many details from the film as you can.

After watching the film, reflect on the following two questions:

3. Which one or two events described in this video do you think were most important in the transformation of Germany from democracy to dictatorship?

4. Which choices made by groups or by individuals seemed to have the greatest consequences?

HANDOUT

DEMOCRACY TO DICTATORSHIP READING ANALYSIS

DIRECTIONS: Read and discuss the reading your group has been assigned, and then respond to the following questions.

1. Write the title of your reading and a short summary (two or three sentences):

Title: ____

2. List the names and date(s) of important events discussed in this reading. Each reading has a different number of events, so you might not use the whole chart.

DATE	EVENT

3. Explain how each of the events listed above contributed to the dismantling of democracy and the establishment of dictatorship in Germany.

4. What does this reading suggest about the values, institutions, and groups that must be protected and strengthened in order to make democracy possible?

READING

SHAPING PUBLIC OPINION

As the Nazis eliminated civil liberties in Germany and opened the first concentration camps to imprison "enemies of the state," they were also trying to win public approval for their government. According to historian Robert Gellately,

> Hitler and his henchmen did not want to cower the German people as a whole into submission, but to win them over by building on popular images, cherished ideals, and long held phobias in the country. . . . [The Nazis] aimed to create and maintain the broadest possible level of popular backing. They expended an enormous amount of energy and resources to track public opinion and to win over people.[1]

The Reich Ministry of Public Enlightenment and Propaganda played a key role in the Nazis' efforts to cultivate favorable public opinion. Propaganda is biased or misleading information that is used to influence public opinion. Hitler created the new ministry on March 13, 1933, and put Joseph Goebbels in charge. It was his job "not just to present the regime and its policies in a positive light, but to generate the impression that the entire German people enthusiastically endorsed everything it did."[2]

To generate excitement and enthusiasm for the Nazi Party and for Hitler himself, Goebbels and his ministry created new festivals and holidays, such as the celebration of Hitler's birthday. They changed street names and other public signage to erase reminders of the Weimar Republic. They organized party rallies and dramatic torch-lit parades to demonstrate public support.

Writing in 1939, journalist Sebastian Haffner described these demonstrations and recalled the effect they had on many Germans.

> [O]ne was permanently occupied and distracted by an unending sequence of celebrations, ceremonies, and national festivities. It started with a huge victory celebration before the elections on March 4 . . . There were mass parades, fireworks, drums, bands, and flags all over Germany, Hitler's voice over thousands of loudspeakers, oaths and vows—all before it was even certain that the elections might not be a setback for the Nazis, which indeed they were. These elections, the last that were ever held in prewar Germany, brought the Nazis only 44 percent of the votes (in the previous elections they had achieved 37 percent). The majority was still against the Nazis.
>
> A week later, Hindenburg abolished the Weimar national flag, which was replaced by the swastika banner and a black, white, and red "temporary national flag." There were daily parades, mass meetings, declarations of gratitude for the liberation of the nation, military music from dawn to dusk, awards ceremonies for heroes, the dedication of flags. . . . Hitler swearing loyalty to something or other for the nth time, bells tolling, a solemn procession to church by the members of the Reichstag, a military parade, swords lowered in salute, children waving flags, and a torchlight parade.

> The colossal emptiness and lack of meaning of these never-ending events was by no means unintentional. The population should become used to cheering and jubilation, even when there was no visible reason for it. . . . Better to celebrate, howl with the wolves, "Heil, Heil!" Besides, people began to enjoy doing so. The weather in March 1933 was glorious. Was it not wonderful to celebrate in the spring sunshine, in squares decked with flags? To merge with the festive crowds and listen to high-sounding patriotic speeches, about freedom and fatherland, exaltation and holy vows?[3]

Goebbels and his ministry also set out to coordinate every form of expression in Germany—from music to radio programs to textbooks, artwork, newspapers, and even sermons—crafting language and imagery carefully to praise Nazi policies and Hitler himself, and to demonize those who the Nazis considered enemies. While the ministry's work included censoring much German art and media, the Nazis also created an environment in which many artists, newspaper editors, and filmmakers censored themselves in order to gain favor with the regime, avoid punishment, or escape the Nazis' attention altogether.[4]

[1] Robert Gellately, *Backing Hitler: Consent and Coercion in Nazi Germany* (Oxford: Oxford University Press, 2001), vii.

[2] Richard J. Evans, *The Third Reich in Power* (New York: Penguin, 2005), 121.

[3] Sebastian Haffner, "Street-Level Coercion," in *How Was It Possible? A Holocaust Reader*, ed. Peter Hayes (Lincoln, NE: University of Nebraska Press, 2015), 122, excerpt from *Defying Hitler: A Memoir*, trans. Oliver Pretzel (New York: Farrar, Straus and Giroux, 2002), 128–29.

[4] Doris Bergen to Facing History and Ourselves, comment on draft manuscript, December 23, 2015.

READING

TARGETING JEWS

From the start, Adolf Hitler and his fellow Nazis were determined to resolve the so-called "Jewish question." In Hitler's words, Nazi leaders were to bring it up "again and again and again, unceasingly. Every emotional aversion, however slight, must be exploited ruthlessly." Julius Streicher, the publisher of an antisemitic newspaper known as *Der Stürmer* (the word means "attacker"), led the way in creating that kind of propaganda, claiming:

> The same Jew who plunged the German people into the bloodletting of the World War, and who committed on it the crime of the November Revolution [Weimar Republic,] is now engaged in stabbing Germany, recovering from its shame and misery, in the back. . . . The Jew is again engaged in poisoning public opinion.[1]

Propaganda was not the only weapon the Nazis used against the Jews. They also relied on terror. On March 9, 1933, just a few days after the elections, Nazi SA storm troopers in Berlin imprisoned dozens of Jewish immigrants from eastern Europe. In Breslau, they attacked Jewish lawyers and judges. On March 13 in Mannheim, they forced Jewish shopkeepers to close their doors. In other towns, they broke into Jewish homes and beat up the people living there.

Although these events were rarely reported in the German press, the foreign press wrote about them regularly. In the United States, many Jews and non-Jews were outraged by the violence. Some called for a boycott of German goods. Their outburst gave the Nazis an excuse for a "defensive action against the Jewish world criminal" on April 1, 1933.

That action—a boycott of Jewish-owned businesses—was the first major public event that specifically targeted Jews not as Communists or Social Democrats but as Jews. It was not a huge success. In some places, Germans showed their disapproval of the boycott by making a point of shopping at Jewish-owned stores on April 1.

Even in places where the boycott took place as planned, the Nazis quickly discovered that it was not always easy to decide if a business was Jewish-owned. There was no legal definition of who was a Jew and who was not. Also, many Jews had non-Jewish business partners, and nearly all had non-Jewish employees. Were those businesses to be closed as well? For example, Tietz, a chain of department stores in Berlin owned by Jews, had more than 14,000 employees, almost all of whom were non-Jews. At a time when unemployment was high and the economy fragile, did the Nazis really want to put those workers out of a job? In the end, the Nazis allowed Tietz to remain open—at least for the time being. A few years later, the owners were forced to turn over their stores to "Aryan" businessmen.

The boycott did succeed, however, in one of its goals: it terrorized Jews throughout Germany. Edwin Landau described what it was like in his hometown in West Prussia. On the Friday before the boycott, he recalled, "one saw the SA [storm troopers] marching through the city with its banners: 'The Jews are our misfortune.' 'Against the Jewish atrocity propaganda abroad.'" He wrote about the day of the boycott:

I took my war decorations, put them on, went into the street, and visited Jewish shops, where at first I was also stopped. But I was seething inside, and most of all I would have liked to shout my hatred into the faces of the barbarians. Hatred, hatred—when had it become a part of me? — It was only a few hours ago that a change had occurred within me. This land and this people that until now I had loved and treasured had suddenly become my enemy. So I was not a German anymore, or I was no longer supposed to be one. That, of course, cannot be settled in a few hours. But one thing I felt immediately: I was ashamed that I had once belonged to this people. I was ashamed about the trust that I had given to so many who now revealed themselves as my enemies. Suddenly the street, too, seemed alien to me; indeed, the whole town had become alien to me. Words do not exist to describe the feelings that I experienced in those hours. Having arrived at home, I approached the one guard whom I knew and who also knew me, and I said to him: "When you were still in your diapers I was already fighting out there for this country." He answered: "You should not reproach me for my youth, sir . . . I've been ordered to stand here." I looked at his young face and thought, he's right. Poor, misguided young people![2]

[1] Quoted in Nora Levin, *The Holocaust: The Destruction of European Jewry 1933–1945* (New York: Schocken, 1973), 46.

[2] Edwin Landau, "My Life before and after Hitler," in *Jewish Life in Germany: Memoirs from Three Centuries*, ed. Monika Richarz, trans. Stella P. Rosenfeld and Sidney Rosenfeld (Bloomington, IN: Indiana University Press, 1991), 310–12.

READING

"RESTORING" GERMANY'S CIVIL SERVICE

On April 7, 1933, a new law, known as the Law for the Restoration of the Professional Civil Service, went into effect. *Civil service* refers to the professionals who work in various agencies of a government, including public education, law enforcement, and more. The law required that all Jews and political opponents of the Nazis who were employed by the government in Germany be fired. The only Jews allowed to keep their positions were veterans, their fathers, and their sons. Similar laws dismissed all Jewish prosecuting attorneys and Jewish doctors who worked in the national health system.

On April 4, when he heard rumors of the new law, President Paul von Hindenburg wrote a letter to Hitler:

> Dear Mr. Chancellor!
>
> Recently, a whole series of cases has been reported to me in which judges, lawyers, and officials of the Judiciary who are disabled war veterans and whose record in office is flawless, have been forcibly sent on leave, and are later to be dismissed for the sole reason that they are of Jewish descent.
>
> It is quite intolerable for me personally . . . that Jewish officials who were disabled in the war should suffer such treatment, [especially] as, with the express approval of the government, I addressed a Proclamation to the German people on the day of the national uprising, March 21, in which I bowed in reverence before the dead of the war and remembered in gratitude the bereaved families of the war dead, the disabled, and my old comrades at the front.
>
> I am certain, Mr. Chancellor, that you share this human feeling, and request you, most cordially and urgently, to look into this matter yourself, and to see to it that there is some uniform arrangement for all branches of the public service in Germany.
>
> As far as my own feelings are concerned, officials, judges, teachers and lawyers who are war invalids, fought at the front, are sons of war dead, or themselves lost sons in the war should remain in their positions unless an individual case gives reason for different treatment. If they were worthy of fighting for Germany and bleeding for Germany, then they must also be considered worthy of continuing to serve the Fatherland. . .

On April 5, Hitler replied to Hindenburg.

> Dear Mr. President!
>
> In a most generous and humane manner you, Mr. Field Marshal, plead the cause of those members of the Jewish people who were once compelled, by the requirements of universal military service, to serve in the war. . . .
>
> But, with the greatest respect, may I point out that members and supporters of my movement, who are Germans, for years were driven from all Government positions, without consideration for their wives and children or their war service. . . . Those responsible for this cruelty were the same Jewish parties which today complain when their supporters are denied the right to official positions, with a thousand times more justification, because they are of little use in these positions but can do limitless harm . . .
>
> Nevertheless, . . . the law in question . . . will provide consideration for those Jews who either served in the war themselves, were disabled in the war, have other merits, or never gave occasion for complaint in the course of a long period of service.
>
> In general, the primary aim of this cleansing process is only to restore a certain sound and natural balance, and, secondly, to remove from official positions of national significance those elements to which one cannot entrust Germany's survival. . . .
>
> I beg you, Mr. President, to believe that I will try to do justice to your noble feelings as far as is possible. I understand your inner motivations and myself, by the way, frequently suffer under the harshness of a fate which forces us to make decisions which, from a human point of view, one would a thousand times rather avoid.
>
> Work on the law in question will proceed as quickly as possible, and I am convinced that this matter, too, will then find the best possible solution.[1]

[1] Yitzhak Arad, Yisrael Gutman, and Abraham Margaliot, eds., *Documents on the Holocaust: Selected Sources on the Destruction of the Jews of Germany and Austria, Poland, and the Soviet Union* (Jerusalem: Yad Vashem, 1987), 37–39.

READING

WHERE THEY BURN BOOKS

On May 6, 1933, the German Student Association announced a nationwide "Action against the Un-German Spirit." At one gathering, Joseph Goebbels told a cheering crowd, "The soul of the German people can again express itself. Those flames not only illuminate the final end of an old era; they light up the new!"[1] Lilian T. Mowrer, an American journalist in Germany, described what happened next:

> I held my breath while he hurled the first volume into the flames: it was like burning something alive. Then students followed with whole armfuls of books, while schoolboys screamed into the microphone their condemnations of this and that author, and as each name was mentioned the crowd booed and hissed. You felt Goebbels's venom behind their denunciations. Children of fourteen mouthing abuse of Heine! Erich Remarque's *All Quiet on the Western Front* received the greatest condemnation . . . it would never do for such an unheroic description of war to dishearten soldiers of the Third Reich.[2]

The mobs also burned the books of Helen Keller, an American author who was a socialist, a pacifist, and the first deaf-blind person to graduate from college. Keller responded: "History has taught you nothing if you think you can kill ideas. . . . You can burn my books and the books of the best minds in Europe, but the ideas in them have seeped through a million channels and will continue to quicken other minds."[3]

[1] William L. Shirer, *The Rise and Fall of the Third Reich: A History of Nazi Germany* (New York: Simon & Schuster, 1990), 241.

[2] Quoted in *Witness to the Holocaust*, ed. Azriel Eisenberg (Cleveland, OH: Pilgrim Press, 1981), 79.

[3] Quoted in Rebecca Onion, "'God Sleepeth Not': Helen Keller's Blistering Letter to Book-Burning German Students," *The Vault* (blog), Slate.com, May 16, 2013, http://www.slate.com/blogs/the_vault/2013/05/16/helen_keller_her_scathing_letter_to_german_students_planning_to_burn_her.html.

READING

ISOLATING HOMOSEXUALS

After taking control of Germany, the Nazis increased their attacks on gay men. Many Germans applauded the move. Homophobia was not uncommon in German society; homosexuals had long been the target of bigotry and discrimination. In 1871, Germany had enacted a provision in the criminal code, known as Paragraph 175, that made homosexual acts a crime. (Several other nations had similar laws at the time.) That law was still on the books, and many homosexual men were harassed or arrested by police throughout the years of the Weimar Republic. Nevertheless, in Berlin and a few larger German cities, tolerance of homosexuality increased in the 1920s and 1930s, and homosexual culture flourished. Many were able to live their lives openly without hiding their sexual orientation. The Reichstag was even considering abolishing Paragraph 175 before the Nazis came to power.[1]

The Nazis believed that homosexual men were "defective" and an obstacle to the goal of creating a master "Aryan" race. They did not embody, in the Nazis' view, the masculinity of the ideal German man. The Nazis also feared that if homosexuals held leadership positions in the Nazi Party or government, they would be vulnerable to manipulation or blackmail by anyone who threatened to expose their sexual orientation. The Nazis were not nearly as concerned about lesbians, who, as women, they presumed would be passive and could be forced to have children.[2]

When Hitler took over in 1933, enforcement of Paragraph 175 was stepped up. A man who lived near Hamburg recalled:

> With one blow a wave of arrests of homosexuals began in our town. One of the first to be arrested was my friend, with whom I had had a relationship since I was 23. One day people from the Gestapo came to his house and took him away. It was pointless to inquire where he might be. If anyone did that, they ran the risk of being similarly detained, because he knew them, and therefore they were also suspect. Following his arrest, his home was searched by Gestapo agents. Books were taken away, note- and address books were confiscated, questions were asked among the neighbors. . . . The address books were the worst. All those who figured in them, or had anything to do with him were arrested and summoned by the Gestapo. Me, too. For a whole year I was summoned by the Gestapo and interrogated at least once every fourteen days or three weeks. . . . After four weeks my friend was released from investigative custody. The [Nazis] could not prove anything against him either. However, the effects of his arrest were terrifying. Hair shorn off, totally confused, he was no longer what he was before. . . . We had to be very careful with all contacts. I had to break off all relations with my friend. We passed each other by on the street, because we did not want to put ourselves in danger. . . . We lived like animals in a wild game park, always sensing the hunters.[3]

[1] Geoffrey J. Giles, "Why Bother About Homosexuals? Homophobia and Sexual Politics in Nazi Germany," lecture, United States Holocaust Memorial Museum Center for Advanced Holocaust Studies, Washington, DC, May 30, 2001, accessed March 18, 2016, https://www.ushmm.org/m/pdfs/20050726-giles.pdf.

[2] Doris L. Bergen, *War and Genocide: A Concise History of the Holocaust* (Lanham, MD: Rowman & Littlefield, 2003), 57.

[3] Quoted in Michael Burleigh and Wolfgang Wippermann, *The Racial State: Germany 1933–1945* (Cambridge, UK: Cambridge University Press, 1991), 194.

READING

PLEDGING ALLEGIANCE

When German president Paul von Hindenburg died on August 2, 1934, Hitler combined the positions of chancellor and president. He was now the führer and Reich chancellor, the head of state, and the chief of the armed forces. In the past, German soldiers had taken this oath:

> I swear loyalty to the Constitution and vow that I will protect the German nation and its lawful establishments as a brave soldier at any time and will be obedient to the President and my superiors.

Now Hitler created a new oath.

> I swear by God this sacred oath, that I will render unconditional obedience to Adolf Hitler, the Führer of the German Reich and people, Supreme Commander of the Armed Forces, and will be ready as a brave soldier to risk my life at any time for this oath.

In his book *The Rise and Fall of the Third Reich*, William Shirer, an American journalist, writes that the new oath "enabled an even greater number of officers to excuse themselves from any personal responsibility for the unspeakable crimes which they carried out on the orders of the Supreme Commander whose true nature they had seen for themselves. . . . One of the appalling aberrations of the German officer corps from this point on rose out of this conflict of 'honor'—a word . . . often on their lips. . . . Later and often, by honoring their oath they dishonored themselves as human beings and trod in the mud the moral code of their corps."[1]

[1] William Shirer, *The Rise and Fall of the Third Reich* (New York: Simon & Schuster, 1960), 227.

READING

DO YOU TAKE THE OATH?

Soldiers were not the only ones required to take the new oath that pledged allegiance to Hitler. One German recalled the day he was asked to pledge loyalty to the regime:

> I was employed in a defense plant (a war plant, of course, but they were always called defense plants). That was the year of the National Defense Law, the law of "total conscription." Under the law I was required to take the oath of fidelity. I said I would not; I opposed it in conscience. I was given twenty-four hours to "think it over." In those twenty-four hours I lost the world. . . .
>
> You see, refusal would have meant the loss of my job, of course, not prison or anything like that. (Later on, the penalty was worse, but this was only 1935.) But losing my job would have meant that I could not get another. Wherever I went I should be asked why I left the job I had, and when I said why, I should certainly have been refused employment. Nobody would hire a "Bolshevik." Of course, I was not a Bolshevik, but you understand what I mean.
>
> I tried not to think of myself or my family. We might have got out of the country in any case, and I could have got a job in industry or education somewhere else.
>
> What I tried to think of was the people to whom I might be of some help later on, if things got worse (as I believed they would). I had a wide friendship in scientific and academic circles, including many Jews, and "Aryans," too, who might be in trouble. If I took the oath and held my job, I might be of help, somehow, as things went on. If I refused to take the oath, I would certainly be useless to my friends, even if I remained in the country. I myself would be in their situation.
>
> The next day, after "thinking it over," I said I would take the oath with the mental reservation, that, by the words with which the oath began, "Ich schwöre bei Gott," "I swear by God," I understood that no human being and no government had the right to override my conscience. My mental reservations did not interest the official who administered the oath. He said, "Do you take the oath?" and I took it. That day the world was lost, and it was I who lost it.
>
> First of all, there is the problem of the lesser evil. Taking the oath was not so evil as being unable to help my friends later on would have been. But the evil of the oath was certain and immediate, and the helping of my friends was in the future and therefore uncertain. I had to commit a positive evil there and then, in the hope of a possible good later on. The good outweighed the evil; but the good was only a hope, the evil a fact. . . . The hope might not have been realized—either for reasons beyond my control or because I became afraid later on or even because I was afraid all the time and was simply fooling myself when I took the oath in the first place . . .

There I was in 1935, a perfect example of the kind of person who, with all his advantages in birth, in education, and in position, rules (or might easily rule) in any country. . . . My education did not help me, and I had a broader and better education than most have had or ever will have. All it did, in the end, was to enable me to rationalize my failure of faith more easily than I might have done if I had been ignorant. And so it was, I think, among educated men generally, in that time in Germany. Their resistance was no greater than other men's.[1]

[1] From Milton Mayer, *They Thought They Were Free: The Germans 1933–45* (Chicago: University of Chicago Press, 1955), 177–81. Reproduced by permission from University of Chicago Press.

READING

REFUSING TO PLEDGE ALLEGIANCE

Joachim Fest's father—a devout Catholic and the headmaster of an elementary school—refused to demonstrate loyalty to the Nazis, even after the new law to "restore" the civil service. He remained active in the Catholic Central Party and the Reichsbanner (a pro-democracy group). Fest describes the consequences his father, a civil servant because he worked in a school, faced for his refusal to show loyalty:

> On April 20, 1933, my father was summoned to Lichtenberg Town Hall . . . and informed by Volz, the state commissar responsible for the exercise of the business of the borough mayor, that he was suspended from public service, effective immediately. When my father asked what he was accused of, the official responded in a sergeant-majorish manner: "You will be informed of that in due course!" But he was a civil servant, objected my father, to which Volz replied, "You can tell our Führer that. He'll be very impressed." . . .
>
> As he was on his way to the exit, all at once the building he knew so well seemed unfamiliar. It was the same with the staff, some of whom he had known for years; suddenly, one after the other, their eyes were avoiding his. At his school, to which he went immediately, it was no different, even in his office; everything from the cupboards to the stationery already seemed to have been replaced. The first person he bumped into was his colleague Markwitz who had clearly already been informed. "Fest, old man!" he said, after my father had spoken a few explanatory words. "Did it have to be like this?" And when my father replied, "Yes, it had to be!," Markwitz objected: "No, don't tell me that! It's something I learned early: there's no 'must' when it comes to stupidity!"
>
> On April 22 . . . my father was summoned again. Remaining seated and without offering my father a chair, the temporary mayor, reading from a prepared text, formally notified him that he was relieved of his duties as headmaster of the Twentieth Elementary School and was suspended until further notice. Given as grounds for the suspension were his senior positions in the [Catholic Center] party and in the Reichsbanner [a pro-democracy group founded during the Weimar years], as well as his "public speeches disparaging the Führer and other high-ranking National Socialists" . . . Under the circumstances there was no longer any guarantee that he would "at all times support without reservation the national state," as the law put it . . . As he spoke these curt words, he continued leafing through my father's file and one of the pages fell to the floor—no doubt intentionally, thought my father. Volz clearly expected my father to pick it up. My father, however, remained motionless, as he later reported; not for one moment did he consider going down on his knees in front of the mayor.

Volz then continued in a noticeably sharper tone. As well as being summarily suspended, my father was required within two days to formally transfer charge of the school to his successor, Markwitz. He would be informed in writing of the details. With a gesture that was part dismissal, part shooing away to the door, the provisional mayor added that for the time being my father was not allowed to take up any employment. Everything proceeded as if according to a plan, said my father, when he came to talk about what happened.[1]

Ricarda Huch, a 70-year-old poet and writer, also refused to pledge allegiance to Hitler. She resigned from the prestigious Prussian Academy of Arts with this letter:

Heidelberg, April 9, 1933

Dear President von Schillings:

Let me first thank you for the warm interest you have taken in having me remain in the Academy. I would very much like you to understand why I cannot follow your wish. That a German's feelings are German, I would consider to be just about self-evident, but the definition of what is German, and what acting in a German manner means—those are things where opinions differ. What the present government prescribes by way of patriotic convictions is not my kind of Germanism. The centralization, the use of compulsion, the brutal methods, the defamation of those who hold different convictions, the boastful self-praise—these are matters which I consider un-German and disastrous. As I consider the divergence between this opinion of mine and that being ordered by the state, I find it impossible to remain in an Academy that is a part of the state. You say that the declaration submitted to me by the Academy would not prevent me from the free expression of my opinions. But "loyal cooperation, in the spirit of the changed historical situation, on matters affecting national and cultural tasks that fall within the jurisdiction of the Academy" requires an agreement with the government's program which in my case does not exist. Besides, I would find no newspaper or magazine that would print an opposition opinion. Thus the right to free expression of opinion would remain quite theoretical. . . .

I hereby resign from the Academy.

S. Ricarda Huch[2]

1 Joachim Fest, *Not I: Memoirs of a German Childhood*, trans. Martin Chalmers (New York: Other Press, 2006), 46–48. Reprinted by permission from Other Press, LLC, and Atlantic Books, UK.

2 Ricarda Huch, "'Not My Kind of Germanism': A Resignation from the Academy," in *The Nazi Years: A Documentary History*, ed. Joachim Remak (Prospect Heights, IL: Waveland Press, 1969), 162.

HANDOUT

FIRST REGULATION TO THE REICH CITIZENSHIP LAW

NOTE: This law, passed on November 14, 1935, amended the original Reich Citizenship Law, passed on September 15, 1935.

Article 3

Only the Reich citizen, as bearer of full political rights, exercises the right to vote in political affairs or can hold public office . . .

Article 4

1. A Jew cannot be a citizen of the Reich. He has no right to vote in political affairs and he cannot occupy public office.

2. Jewish [government] officials will retire as of December 31, 1935 . . .

Article 5

1. A Jew is anyone who is descended from at least three grandparents who are racially full Jews . . .

2. A Jew is also one who is descended from two full Jewish parents, if (a) he belonged to the Jewish religious community at the time this law was issued, or joined the community later, (b) he was married to a Jewish person, at the time the law was issued, or married one subsequently, (c) he is the offspring of a marriage with a Jew, in the sense of Section I, which was contracted after the Law for the Protection of German Blood and German Honor became effective, (d) he is the offspring of an extramarital relationship with a Jew, according to Section I, and will be born out of wedlock after July 31, 1936 . . .[1]

[1] Jeremy Noakes and Geoffrey Pridham, eds., *Documents on Nazism 1919–1945* (New York: Viking Press, 1974), 463–67.

HANDOUT

LAW FOR THE PROTECTION OF GERMAN BLOOD AND HONOR, PART 1

Moved by the understanding that purity of German blood is the essential condition for the continued existence of the German people, and inspired by the inflexible determination to ensure the existence of the German nation for all time, the Reichstag has unanimously adopted the following law, which is promulgated herewith:

Article 1

1. Marriages between Jews and subjects of the state of German or related blood are forbidden. Marriages nevertheless concluded are invalid, even if concluded abroad to circumvent this law . . .

Article 2

Extramarital relations between Jews and subjects of the state of German or related blood are forbidden.

Article 5

1. Any person who violates the prohibition under Article 1 will be punished with a prison sentence.

2. A male who violates the prohibition under Article 2 will be punished with a jail term or a prison sentence.[1]

[1] "Reich Citizenship Law of September 15, 1935," trans. by the United States Holocaust Memorial Museum, https://www.ushmm.org/wlc/en/article.php?ModuleId=10007903.

HANDOUT

LAW FOR THE PROTECTION OF GERMAN BLOOD AND HONOR, PART 2

Moved by the understanding that purity of German blood is the essential condition for the continued existence of the German people, and inspired by the inflexible determination to ensure the existence of the German nation for all time, the Reichstag has unanimously adopted the following law, which is promulgated herewith:

Article 3

Jews may not employ in their households female subjects of the state of German or related blood who are under 45 years old.

Article 4

1. Jews are forbidden to fly the Reich or national flag or display Reich colors.

2. They are, on the other hand, permitted to display the Jewish colors. The exercise of this right is protected by the state.

Article 5

Any person violating the provisions under Articles 3 or 4 will be punished with a jail term of up to one year and a fine, or with one or the other of these penalties . . .[1]

[1] "Reich Citizenship Law of September 15, 1935," trans. by the United States Holocaust Memorial Museum, https://www.ushmm.org/wlc/en/article.php?ModuleId=10007903.

READING

DISCOVERING JEWISH BLOOD

The Nuremberg Laws turned Jews from German citizens into "residents of Germany." The laws transformed the lives of Jews all over Germany, including thousands of people who had not previously known their families had Jewish heritage. Among them were Marianne Schweitzer and her siblings.

> Although we were not a churchgoing family, we observed Christmas and Easter in the traditional ways and belonged to the Lutheran church. My parents, my three siblings and I were all baptized and I took confirmation classes with Martin Niemöller, the former U-boat commander and his brother who substituted when Martin was in prison for anti-Nazi activities.
>
> It was in 1932 that my [older] sister Rele provoked my father to reveal our Jewish ancestry for the first time. She played the violin and rejected a violin teacher because he "looked too Jewish." Our father had responded in a rather convoluted way by saying, "Don't you know that your grandmother came from the same people as Jesus . . . ?"
>
> Our mother's side, the Körtes, were "Aryan" by Hitler's standards. But our father's parents, Eugen Schweitzer and Algunde Hollaender were Jews born in Poland who had been baptized as adults. My father and his two brothers were considered Jews by Hitler's laws. Though all were married to non-Jewish wives, our lives were dramatically changed. The whole family was devastated and worried about our future. My mother's "Aryan" side stood by my father. My Körte grandmother said, "If Hitler is against Ernst [my father], I am against Hitler."
>
> We heard no anti-Jewish remarks at home, but the antisemitism of that time was so pervasive and the images in periodicals such as *Der Stürmer* so ugly, that Rele later wrote of her shock at learning her relation to "monsters." She considered herself "the typical German girl with blond, curly hair." I took the news more in stride. I was happy to be able to stay in school and glad not to be eligible to join Hitler Youth. . . .
>
> In September of 1935, the Nuremberg Laws were introduced. My "Jewish" father was barred from treating "Aryan" patients, employing "Aryans," attending concerts or the theater, or using public transportation. Rele had passed her Abitur, the certification of completing a high school degree, but as a Mischling, was ineligible to attend university. She couldn't marry her "Aryan" boyfriend Hans, a medical student.[1]

The Schweitzers were certainly not the only Germans to be penalized for having "Jewish blood." By 1935, explains historian Martin Gilbert,

> The search for Jews, and for converted Jews, to be driven out of their jobs was continuous. On 5 September 1935 the SS newspaper published the names of eight half-Jews and converted Jews, all of the Evangelical Lutheran faith, who had been "dismissed without notice and deprived of any further opportunity of acting as organists in Christian churches." From these dismissals, the newspaper commented, "It can be seen that the Reich Chamber of Music is taking steps to protect the church from pernicious influence."[2]

[1] Marianne Schweitzer, afterword to Melita Maschmann, *Account Rendered: A Dossier on My Former Self*, trans. Geoffrey Strachan (Cambridge, MA: Plunkett Lake Press, 2013).

[2] Martin Gilbert, *The Holocaust: A History of the Jews of Europe During the Second World War* (New York: Holt, 1985), 47.

IMAGE

HITLER YOUTH PROPAGANDA

This 1935 poster promotes the Hitler Youth by stating: "Youth serves the Führer! All ten-year-olds into the Hitler Youth."

akg-images

HANDOUT
YOUTH IN NAZI GERMANY READING SET 1

Schooling for the National Community

Gregor Ziemer was a teacher and headmaster at the American School in Berlin (a school for the children of American citizens living in Germany) for most of the 1930s. During this time, Ziemer toured German schools and eventually wrote a book called *Education for Death*, which was first published in 1941. In it, Ziemer describes the schools he visited:

> A teacher is not spoken of as a teacher (*Lehrer*) but an *Erzieher*. The word suggests an iron disciplinarian who does not instruct but commands, and whose orders are backed up with force if necessary.
>
> Matters of the spirit are frankly and energetically belittled. Physical education, education for action, is alone worthy of the Nazi teacher's attention. All else can be dismissed as non-essential . . .
>
> The Nazi schools are no place for weaklings. All children must, of course, finish the primary school before they are ten; but after that the schools are proving-grounds for the Party. Those who betray any weakness of body or have not the capacities for absolute obedience and submission must be expelled. . . .
>
> The regime draws a sharp distinction between girls, inherently weak, and boys, natural exponents of strength. Boys and girls have nothing in common. Their aims, their purposes in life, are fundamentally different. Boys will become soldiers; girls will become breeders. Co-educational schools are manifestations of decadent democracies and hence are taboo.
>
> [Dr. Bernhard Rust, the Nazi Minister of Education] decrees that in Nazi schools the norm is physical education. After that, German, biology, science, mathematics, and history are for the boys; eugenics and home economics for the girls. Other subjects are permissible if they are taught to promote Nazi ideas. Spiritual education is definitely unimportant.[1]

History and science were the subjects most influenced by Nazi ideology. Soon after Hitler took power, a new course in "race science" was added to the curriculum in every German school. But racial instruction was not limited to a single course. It was included in all classes, even arithmetic. One book, titled *Germany's Fall and Rise—Illustrations Taken from Arithmetic Instruction in the Higher Grades of Elementary School*, asks, "The Jews are aliens in Germany—in 1933 there were 66,060,000 inhabitants of the German Reich, of whom 499,682 were Jews. What is the percentage of aliens?"[2]

[1] Gregor Ziemer, *Education for Death: The Making of the Nazi* (Oxford: Oxford University Press, 1941), 15–16.

[2] Ziemer, *Education for Death*, 16.

Indoctrination

Hede von Nagel grew up in Nazi Germany. She wrote of her childhood:

> As my parents' second daughter, I was a great disappointment to my father, who wanted to produce sons for the Führer and the nation—and, because he was of the nobility, to carry on the family name.
>
> He was furious that, unlike my fair-haired older sister, who looked so Nordic, I had been cursed with auburn hair and dark brown eyes. Then came a third child, this time a male, but he was a dark-eyed redhead—another let down for my patriotic father. Only when another son was born and proved to be the very model of a tow-headed, blue-eyed Aryan was my father satisfied. "At last," he said, "the child I wanted."
>
> Our parents taught us to raise our arms and say "Heil Hitler" before we said "Mama." This type of indoctrination was universal. Children experienced it in kindergarten, at home—everywhere. We grew up believing that Hitler was a super-god, and Germany an anointed nation. . . .
>
> At the same time, our parents and teachers trained my sister and me to be the unquestioning helpmates of men; as individuals, we had no right to our own opinion, no right to speak up.[1]

[1] Hede von Nagel, "The Nazi Legacy—Fearful Silence for Their Children," *Boston Globe*, October 23, 1977.

Joining the Hitler Youth

Alfons Heck was an enthusiastic participant in the Nazi Youth organizations. In a memoir written many years after World War II, Heck reflected on what made him want to join:

> Far from being forced to enter the ranks of the Jungvolk, I could barely contain my impatience and was, in fact, accepted before I was quite 10. It seemed like an exciting life, free from parental supervision, filled with "duties" that seemed sheer pleasure. Precision marching was something one could endure for hiking, camping, war games in the field, and a constant emphasis on sports. . . . To a degree, our pre-war activities resembled those of the Boy Scouts, with much more emphasis on discipline and political indoctrination. There were the paraphernalia and the symbols, the pomp and the mysticism, very close in feeling to religious rituals. One of the first significant demands was the so-called . . . "test of courage," which was usually administered after a six-month period of probation. The members of my Schar, a platoon-like unit of about 40–50 boys, were required to dive off the three-meter board—about 10 feet high—head first in the town's swimming pool. There were some stinging belly flops, but the pain was worth it when our Fahnleinführer, the 15-year-old leader of Fahnlein (literally "little flag"), a company-like unit of about 160 boys, handed us the coveted dagger with its inscription Blood and Honor. From that moment on we were fully accepted.[1]

[1] Alfons Heck, *A Child of Hitler: Germany in the Days When God Wore a Swastika* (Phoenix, AZ: Renaissance House, 1985), 9.

Disillusionment in the Hitler Youth

Hans Scholl, who later founded the White Rose resistance movement with his sister Sophie and was executed by the Nazis, was at one point a member of the Hitler Youth. His sister Inge Scholl describes how Hans slowly became disillusioned with the group:

> Hans had assembled a collection of folk songs, and his young charges loved to listen to him singing, accompanying himself on his guitar . . .
>
> But some time later a peculiar change took place in Hans; he was no longer the same . . . His songs were forbidden, the leader had told him. And when he had laughed at this, they threatened him with disciplinary action. Why should he not be permitted to sing these beautiful songs? Only because they had been created by other peoples? . . . [T]his depressed him, and his usual carefree spirit began to wane.
>
> At this particular time he was given a very special assignment.
>
> He was to carry the flag of his troop to the party's national rally at Nuremberg. He was overjoyed. But when he returned we hardly dared trust our eyes. He looked tired, and on his face lay a great disappointment . . . gradually we learned that the youth movement which had been held up to him as an ideal image was in reality something totally different from what he had imagined the Hitler Youth to be. Their drill and uniformity had been extended into every sphere of personal life. But he had always believed that every boy should develop his own special talents . . .
>
> Ultimately it came to an open break.
>
> One evening, as they stood with their flag in formation for inspection by a higher leader, something unheard-of happened. The visiting leader suddenly ordered the tiny standard-bearer, a frolicsome twelve-year-old lad, to give up the flag. "You don't need a special flag. Just keep the one that has been prescribed for all." Hans was deeply disturbed. Since when? Didn't the troop leader know what this special flag meant to its standard-bearer?
>
> Once more the leader ordered the boy to give up the flag. He stood quiet and motionless. Hans knew what was going on in the little fellow's mind and that he would not obey. When the high leader in a threatening voice ordered the little fellow for the third time, Hans saw the flag waver slightly. He could no longer control himself. He stepped out of line and slapped the visiting leader's face. From then on he was no longer the standard-bearer.[1]

[1] Inge Scholl, *Students Against Tyranny: The Resistance of the White Rose, Munich, 1942–1943*, trans. Arthur R. Schultz (Middletown, CT: Wesleyan University Press, 1970), 7–10. Reproduced by permission from Wesleyan University Press.

HANDOUT

YOUTH IN NAZI GERMANY READING SET 2

Please note that this reading contains dehumanizing language. We have chosen to include it in order to honestly communicate the harmful language of the time; however, dehumanizing language should not be spoken or read aloud during class.

Youth on the Margins, Part 1

When Elizabeth Dopazo and her brother were very young, their parents were sent to concentration camps because of their religious beliefs; they were Jehovah's Witnesses whose faith required that they pledge allegiance only to God. Jehovah's Witnesses therefore refused to say "Heil Hitler" as a matter of religious conviction. After their parents were arrested, seven-year-old Elizabeth and her six-year-old brother went to live with their grandparents. Elizabeth later recalled:

> We had to quickly change our way of speaking so maybe we wouldn't be so noticeable. In school right away it started, you see. We had to raise our right arm and say "Heil Hitler" and all that sort of thing and then we didn't do it a few times. A few times was all right. You can drop a handkerchief, you can do a little something, but quickly they look and they say, "Ah, you're different and you're new in the school." So you're watched a little more closely. You might get one or two children who'd tell on you but it was rare. The teacher would bring you to the front of the class and say "Why don't you say Heil Hitler?" and you were shaking already because you knew, unlike other children, if you told them the real reason there'd be trouble. For us to say "Heil Hitler" and praise a person would be against our belief. We shouldn't because we had already pledged our allegiance to God and that's it. So we could stand and be respectful to the government, but we were not to participate in adulation for political figures. . . .
>
> Later, around age twelve or thirteen, we joined the Hitler Youth, which we actually didn't want to do, but the Gestapo came to my grandparents' house, just like you've seen in the movies with the long leather coats on and they stood at the front door and they were saying, "Your grandchildren have to join the Hitler Youth and if they don't by Thursday we will take stronger measures." After they'd left we told our grandparents we'll join tomorrow, even if we hate all that stuff. They agreed we'd better do it and we very quickly donned those uniforms. . . .
>
> As time went on, my brother, when he was thirteen or fourteen, sort of was swayed. You know, you have to believe in something. He wanted to be a German officer and said our father had been wrong all along and that we went to the dogs for our father's beliefs. He [our father] died for his ideals and where are we? [My brother] was very angry. I was too, but not as much. I was torn between what would be the good thing to do and what would not. . . . [1]

[1] Elizabeth Dopazo, "Reminiscences," unpublished interview, 1981, Facing History and Ourselves.

Comradeship

In 1938, a boy named Hans Wolf wrote a story about his experiences in the Hitler Youth that was published in a school textbook. The story was called "Comradeship." It begins:

> It was a hot day and we had far to march. The sun was burning down on the heath, which was bereft of trees. The sand was glistening, I was tired. My feet were hurting in those new walking shoes, every step was hurting and all I could think about was rest, water, and shade. I clenched my teeth to keep walking. I was the youngest, and this was my first outing. In front of me strode Rudolf, the leader. He was tall and strong. His backpack was heavy and pressed down on his shoulders. Rudolf carried the bread for us six boys, the cooking pot, and a pile of books, from which he would read us wonderfully thrilling stories, at night in the hostel. My backpack only contained a shirt, a couple of sneakers, washing utensils, and some cooking gear, apart from a tarpaulin for rainy days and straw beds. And yet I thought I could not lug this backpack any longer. My comrades all were somewhat older and had camping experience. They hardly felt the heat and hardship of the march. Every now and then they would sigh and drink lukewarm coffee from their canteens. More and more, I remained behind, even though I tried to make up for my slack by running. Suddenly Rudolf turned around. He stopped and watched me crawling up to him from a distance, while our comrades continued in the direction of a few trees on the horizon. "Tired?" Rudolf asked me, kindly. Ashamed, I had to say yes. Slowly, we walked side by side. I was limping. But I did not want to let on to Rudolf. When we got to a juniper bush, the leader sat down and said: "For a little rest!" Relieved, I threw myself down. I did not want to talk, for I was shy. Rudolf gave me something to drink. I thanked him and leaned back comfortably, glad to be able to stretch my aching feet, and before I knew it I was sleeping. . . . When we resumed our march, my feet hurt much less and my backpack did not press down on me so. I was very glad about that.[1]

[1] Hans Wolf, "Comradeship," trans. Michael H. Kater, in Michael H. Kater, Hitler Youth (Cambridge, MA: Harvard University Press, 2004), 13–14.

"Heil Hitler!": Lessons of Daily Life

In 1938, writer Erika Mann published a book called *School for Barbarians: Education Under the Nazis*. Mann had emigrated from Germany to the United States in 1937. Her book criticized the Nazis' efforts to shape young people's ideas and feelings. In it, she describes how daily life in Germany was a kind of "school" that educated children in accordance with Nazi ideals:

> Every child says "Heil Hitler!" from 50 to 150 times a day . . . The formula is required by law; if you meet a friend on the way to school, you say it; study periods are opened and closed with "Heil Hitler!"; "Heil Hitler!" says the postman, the street-car conductor, the girl who sells you notebooks at the stationery store; and if your parents' first words when you come home for lunch are not "Heil Hitler!" they have been guilty of a punishable offense and can be denounced. "Heil Hitler!" they shout in the Jungvolk and Hitler Youth. "Heil Hitler!" cry the girls in the League of German Girls. Your evening prayers must close with "Heil Hitler!" if you take your devotions seriously . . .
>
> . . . You leave the house in the morning, "Heil Hitler" on your lips; and on the stairs of your apartment house you meet the Blockwart [block warden]. A person of great importance and some danger, the Blockwart has been installed by the government as a Nazi guardian. He controls the block, reporting on it regularly, checking up on the behavior of its residents . . . All the way down the street, the flags are waving, every window colored with red banners, and the black swastika in the middle of each. You don't stop to ask why; it's bound to be some national event . . . Only the Jews are exempted under the strict regulation. Jews are not Germans; they do not belong to the "Nation," they can have no "national events." . . .
>
> There are more placards as you continue past hotels, restaurants, indoor swimming pools, to school. They read "No Jews allowed"—"Jews not desired here"—"Not for Jews." And what do you feel? Agreement? Pleasure? Disgust? Opposition? You don't feel any of these. You don't feel anything, you've seen these placards for almost five years. This is a habit, it is all perfectly natural, of course Jews aren't allowed here. Five years in the life of a child of nine—that's his life, after four years of infancy, his whole personal, conscious existence . . . [1]

[1] Erika Mann, School for Barbarians: Education Under the Nazis (Mineola, NY: Dover Publications, 1938), 21–24. Reproduced by permission from Dover Publications

Rejecting Nazism

Some German young people refused to join Nazi youth organizations. One group who refused to join called themselves the *Swing-Jugend* ("swing kids") after a style of American jazz music and dancing they loved. Historian Richard Bessel describes the "swing kids":

> The swing youth were not anti-fascist in a political sense—their behavior was indeed emphatically anti-political—both Nazi slogans and traditional nationalism were of profound indifference to them. They sought their counter-identity in what they saw as the "slovenly" culture of . . . England and America. They accepted Jews and "half-Jews" into their groups . . . and gave ovations to visiting bands from Belgium and Holland.[1]

A Hitler Youth report on a 1940 swing festival attended by more than 500 teenagers in Hamburg describes the kind of behavior that upset Nazi officials:

> The dancers made an appalling sight. None of the couples danced normally; there was only swing of the worst sort. Sometimes two boys danced with one girl; sometimes several formed a circle, linking arms and jumping, slapping hands, even rubbing the backs of their heads together; and then, bent double, with the top half of the body hanging loosely down, long hair flopping into the face, they dragged themselves round practically to their knees. When the band played a rumba, the dancers went into wild ecstasy. They all leaped around and mumbled the chorus in English. The band played wilder and wilder numbers; none of the players was sitting any longer, they all "jitterbugged" on the stage like wild animals. Frequently boys could be observed dancing together, without exception with two cigarettes in the mouth, one in each corner . . . [2]

[1] Richard Bessel, Life in the Third Reich (Oxford: Oxford University Press, 1987), 39.

[2] Bessel, Life in the Third Reich, 37.

Youth on the Margins, Part 2

Daily life in school was difficult for a boy named Frank, one of two Jewish students in a school in Breslau in the mid-1930s. He recalled:

> People started to pick on me, "a dirty Jew," and all this kind of thing. And we started to fight. . . . There was my friend, and he was one class above me, he fought in every break. . . . I started to fight, too, because they insulted too much or they started to fight, whatever it was.
>
> We were very isolated, and one order came after another. . . . [One] order says all Jews must greet with the German greeting. The German greeting was "Heil Hitler" and raising your hand. Then the next order came out, and it says the Jews are not allowed to greet people with the "Heil Hitler" signal. Okay, so, in Germany you had to greet every teacher. When you see a teacher on the street, you had to respect them and you had to greet him—you had to bow down. . . .
>
> Now we were in an impossible situation, because when we went up the stairs and we saw one teacher, and we said "Heil Hitler." And he turned around. "Aren't you a Jew? You're not allowed to greet me with 'Heil Hitler.'" But if I didn't greet him at all, then the next teacher would say "Aren't you supposed to greet [me with] 'Heil Hitler'?" And this was always accompanied with a punishment. . . . Not all of them but some of them, the teachers that knew me and would pick on me—they'd punish me, put me in a corner, or humiliate me in one way or another. . . .

HANDOUT

KRISTALLNACHT: THE NOVEMBER 1938 POGROMS VIEWING GUIDE

DIRECTIONS: In this video, scholars discuss the events of Kristallnacht ("The Night of Broken Glass"), a series of violent attacks against Jews in Germany, Austria, and part of Czechoslovakia in November 1938. As you watch the film, record notes that help you answer the first two questions on this handout. Then respond to the third question after you have finished viewing the film.

1. What did Jews experience during and immediately after Kristallnacht?

2. What do you imagine other Germans would have seen and experienced that night and in the following days?

3. To what extent was Kristallnacht similar to what had come before? How was Kristallnacht different?

HANDOUT

KRISTALLNACHT TESTIMONY VIEWING GUIDE

1. While watching Elsbeth Lewin's testimony, write down a phrase or sentence that resonates with you.

2. After watching Elsbeth's testimony, write a word or a short phrase that describes how you felt while listening to her story.

3. What can you learn about Kristallnacht from the personal testimony of Elsbeth Lewin that you could not learn from other sources, such as readings or videos, that focus on the historical aspects of the event?

HANDOUT

DECISION-MAKING IN TIMES OF FEAR AND CRISIS

DIRECTIONS: After finishing your assigned reading with your group, work together to complete the first three columns of the graphic organizer on the next page together. Do not write anything in the fourth column until your teacher directs you to do so.

After your group has finished the reading and the first three columns of the chart, discuss the following question to prepare for the class discussion:

What does this source suggest about the variety of ways humans might respond to fear and crisis?

Name/Position	**Reaction to Kristallnacht** *How did this person react to Kristallnacht?* *What choices did they make?*	**Motivating Factors** *What factors may have motivated this person and/or influenced their choices?* *How might this person's universe of obligation influence their choices?*	**Label this person's actions.**
Wilehm · Student	Help a jewish store - to stand with a local vendor · followed his conscience	His mother raised him right - Love thy neighbor	- Courageous · Conscience - Neighborly -

Name/Position	**Reaction to Kristallnacht** *How did this person react to Kristallnacht?* *What choices did they make?*	**Motivating Factors** *What factors may have motivated this person and/or influenced their choices?* *How might this person's universe of obligation influence their choices?*	**Label this person's actions.**

READING

THE NIGHT OF THE POGROM

Hugo Moses described what he experienced on Kristallnacht and in the days that followed:

> On the evening of 9 November 1938, the SA brown-shirts and the SS black-shirts met in bars to celebrate the fifteenth anniversary of [the Nazis'] failed putsch in Munich. Around eleven o'clock in the evening, I came home from a Jewish aid organization meeting and I can testify that most of the "German people" who a day later the government said were responsible for what happened that night lay peacefully in bed that evening. Everywhere lights had been put out, and nothing suggested that in the following hours such terrible events would take place.
>
> Even the uniformed party members were not in on the plan; the order to destroy Jewish property came shortly before they moved from the bars to the Jewish houses. (I have this information from the brother of an SS man who took an active part in the pogroms.)
>
> At 3 a.m. sharp, someone insistently rang at the door to my apartment. I went to the window and saw that the streetlights had been turned off. Nonetheless, I could make out a transport vehicle out of which emerged about twenty uniformed men. I recognized only one of them, a man who served as the leader; the rest came from other localities and cities and were distributed over the district in accordance with marching orders. I called out to my wife: "Don't be afraid, they are party men; please keep calm." Then I went to the door in my pajamas and opened it.
>
> A wave of alcohol hit me, and the mob forced its way into the home. A leader pushed by me and yanked the telephone off the wall. A leader of the SS men, green-faced with drunkenness, cocked his revolver as I watched and then held it to my forehead and slurred: "Do you know why we've come here, you swine?" I replied, "No," and he went on, "Because of the outrageous act committed in Paris, for which you are also to blame. If you even try to move, I'll shoot you like a pig." I kept quiet and stood, my hands behind my back, in the ice-cold [draft] coming in the open door. An SA man, who must have had a little human feeling, whispered to me: "Keep still. Don't move." During all this time and for another twenty minutes, the drunken SS leader fumbled threateningly with his revolver near my forehead. An inadvertent movement on my part or a clumsy one on his and my life would have been over. If I live to be a hundred, I will never forget that brutish face and those dreadful minutes.
>
> In the meantime, about ten uniformed men had invaded my house. I heard my wife cry: "What do you want with my children? You'll touch the children over my dead body!" Then I heard only the crashing of overturned furniture, the breaking of glass and the trampling of heavy boots. Weeks later, I was still waking from restless sleep, still hearing that crashing, hammering, and striking. We will never forget that night. After about half an hour, which seemed to me an eternity, the brutish drunks left

> our apartment, shouting and bellowing. The leader blew a whistle and as his subordinates stumbled past him, fired his revolver close to my head, two shots to the ceiling. I thought my eardrums had burst but I stood there like a wall. (A few hours later I showed a police officer the two bullet holes.) The last SA man who left the building hit me on the head so hard with the walking stick he had used to destroy my pictures that a fortnight later the swelling was still perceptible. As he went out, he shouted at me: "There you are, you Jewish pig. Have fun." . . .
>
> Towards dawn, a police officer appeared in order to determine whether there was any damage visible from the outside, such as broken window glass or furniture thrown out into the street. Shaking his head, he said to us, as I showed him the bullet holes from the preceding night: "It's a disgrace to see all this. It wouldn't have happened if we hadn't had to stay in our barracks." As he left, the officer said, "I hope it's the last time this will happen to you."

Two hours later, another police officer appeared and told Moses, "I'm sorry, but I have to arrest you."

> I said to him, "I have never broken the law; tell me why you are arresting me." The officer: "I have been ordered to arrest all Jewish men. Don't make it so hard for me, just follow me." My wife accompanied me to the police station. . . .
>
> At the police station, the officers were almost all nice to us. Only one officer told my wife: "Go home. You may see your husband again after a few years of forced labor in the concentration camp, if he's still alive." Another officer, who had been at school with me, said to his comrade: "Man, don't talk such nonsense." To my wife he said: "Just go home now, you'll soon have your husband back." A few hours later my little boy came to see me again. The experiences of that terrible night and my arrest were too much for the little soul, and he kept weeping and looking at me as if I were about to be shot. The police officer I knew well took the child by the hand and said to me: "I'll take the child to my office until you are taken away. If the boy saw that, he'd never forget it for the rest of his life."[1]

After several weeks in prison, Moses was released, thanks to the wife of an "Aryan" acquaintance. Soon after, he and his family managed to leave Germany. Moses told his story for the first time in 1940, just a year and a half after the pogrom. He refused to reveal the name of his town or the identities of those who helped him, because he did not want to endanger those left behind.

[1] Uta Gerhardt and Thomas Karlauf, eds., *The Night of Broken Glass: Eyewitness Accounts of Kristallnacht* (Cambridge, UK: Polity Press, 2012), 21–23. Reproduced by permission from Polity Press.

READING

OPPORTUNISM DURING KRISTALLNACHT

Despite Gestapo chief Heinrich Müller's instructions to state police that plundering be held to a minimum, the theft of goods, property, and money from Jews by German police, SS members, and civilians amid the chaos of Kristallnacht was widespread.

German newspapers reported the looting of and theft from Jewish-owned businesses. According to Berlin's *Daily Herald* newspaper, "The great shopping centers looked as though they had suffered an air raid . . . Showcases were torn from the walls, furniture broken, electric signs smashed to fragments." *The News Chronicle* newspaper, also from Berlin, reported looters "smashing with peculiar care the windows of jewellery shops and, sniggering, stuffing into their pockets the trinkets and necklaces that fell on the pavements."[1]

In Vienna, Helga Milberg, who was eight years old during Kristallnacht, recalled that all of the goods and equipment from her father's butcher shop were stolen during the pogrom. "My father saw that the other storekeepers had helped themselves to everything," she wrote.[2] According to historian Martin Gilbert, when a British reporter asked a Nazi official about the widespread theft of goods from Jewish businesses during Kristallnacht in Vienna, the official responded:

> "We began seizing goods from Jewish shops because sooner or later they would have been nationalised [confiscated by the government] anyway." The goods thus seized, the official added, "will be used to compensate us for at least part of the damage which the Jews have been doing for years to the German people."[3]

Gilbert also describes how Kurt Füchsl's family lost their home.

> Seven-year-old Kurt Füchsl was bewildered by the events of Kristallnacht, and by being forced to leave home with his family early on the morning of November 10. He later recalled: "What happened, as recounted to me by my Mother, was that an interior decorator had taken a picture of our beautiful living room and displayed the picture of our apartment in his shop window. A Frau [Mrs.] Januba saw the picture and heard that we were Jewish. She came around to the apartment and asked if it was for sale. She was told it wasn't, but a few days later, on the morning of Kristallnacht, she came back with some officers and said, 'This apartment is now mine.' She showed a piece of paper with a swastika stamped on it and told us that we would have to leave by six that evening." Kurt Füchsl's mother protested to the officers who were accompanying Frau Januba that she had a sick child at home who was already asleep. "All right," they told her, "but you have to get out by six in the morning."[4]

German officials also stole cash from Jewish businesses and families. Two weeks after Kristallnacht, Margarete Drexler wrote the following letter to the Gestapo, requesting the return of the money officials had taken from her home in Mannheim, Germany:

> Mannheim, 24 November 1938
>
> Margarete Drexler, Landau Pfalz Suedring St. 10
>
> To the Secret State Police Landau (Pfalz) The sum of 900 Marks in cash was confiscated from me in the course of the action of 10 November. I herewith request to act for the return of my money, as I need it urgently for me and my child's livelihood. I hope that my request will be granted, as my husband died as a result of his injuries during the war — he fought and died for his fatherland with extreme courage — and I am left without any income. Until recent years you could have found a photo of my husband on the wall next to the picture of Generalfeldmarschall [Paul] von Hindenburg in the canteen of the 23 Infantry regiment in Landau. This was done to honour his high military performance. His medals and decorations prove that he fought with great courage and honour. He received: The Iron Cross First Class, The Iron Cross Second Class, The Military Order of Merit Fourth Class with swords. The Military Order of Sanitation 2 class with a blue-white ribbon. This ribbon is usually bestowed only upon recipients of the Max Joseph Order, which accepts only members of the nobility. I can only hope that as a widow of such a man, so honoured by his country, my request for the return of my property will not be in vain.
>
> With German greetings,
> (signed) Frau Margarete Drexler
>
> Widow of reserve staff surgeon
> Dr. Hermann Drexler[5]

In 1940, Drexler was arrested and imprisoned in a concentration camp in France, where she died.

[1] Martin Gilbert, *Kristallnacht: Prelude to Destruction* (New York: HarperCollins, 2006), 46–47.

[2] Gilbert, *Kristallnacht: Prelude to Destruction*, 54.

[3] Gilbert, *Kristallnacht: Prelude to Destruction*, 59.

[4] Gilbert, *Kristallnacht: Prelude to Destruction*, 62.

[5] Yad Vashem, "Looting during 'Crystal Night,'" accessed June 29, 2016, http://www.yadvashem.org/odot_pdf/Microsoft%20Word%20-%203238.pdf.

READING

A FAMILY RESPONDS TO KRISTALLNACHT

Please note that this reading contains dehumanizing language. We have chosen to include it in order to honestly communicate the harmful language of the time; however, dehumanizing language should not be spoken or read aloud during class.

Marie Kahle (a teacher), her husband (a university professor and Lutheran pastor), and their sons witnessed the events of Kristallnacht in the city of Bonn and the effects those events had on their Jewish neighbors and colleagues. Marie Kahle wrote about the choices she and her family made the next day:

> On 10 November, 1938, at 11:30 in the morning, the wife of a Jewish colleague came to me and reported that both the synagogues in Bonn had been set on fire and that SS men had destroyed the Jewish shops, to which I replied: "That can't be true!" She gave me a manuscript to keep, her husband's life work. Then one of my sons brought the same news.
>
> My third son immediately went, without my knowing it, to a Jewish clockmaker's shop, helped the man's wife hide a few things and brought home a chest with the most valuable jewelry and time-pieces. Then he went to a chocolate shop, warned the owner and helped her move tea, coffee, cocoa, etc. to a room in the very back of the building. While three SS men were destroying everything in the front of the shop, he slipped out the back door with a suitcase full of securities and rode home with it on his bicycle. Later on, he spent weeks selling these hidden things to our acquaintances and thus made money for the two shop owners that the Gestapo knew nothing about. A Jewish colleague of my husband's stayed with us all day long on 10 November and thus avoided being arrested.
>
> From 11 November on, my sons worked furiously to help the Jewish shopkeepers clear out their shops. I couldn't take part in this myself because I did not want to endanger my husband's position. I could only visit the poor people. During one of these visits, my eldest son and I were surprised by a policeman, who wrote down my name. The consequence was a newspaper article . . . for 17 November 1938 headed "This is a betrayal of the people: Frau Kahle and her son help the Jewess Goldstein clear out."
>
> On the basis of this newspaper article, my husband was immediately suspended and he was forbidden to enter . . . the university buildings. My eldest son was also forbidden to enter the university. He was convicted by a disciplinary court. . . . During

the night, our house was attacked. Window panes were broken, etc. . . . The police came a short time later but went away again immediately. One of the policemen advised me to look out into the street: there, we found written in large red letters on the pavement: "Traitors to the People! Jew-lovers!" We washed the writing away with turpentine.

However, since the people were constantly coming back in their car, I openly rode away on my bicycle. I did not want to be beaten to death in front of my children and I was also only a danger to my family. I found shelter in a small Catholic convent, where the nuns were kind enough to look after me and my youngest child. During the interrogation by the Gestapo a few days later, I was asked whether I knew the license number of the car whose occupants had made the attack. When I said "no", I was released. As I came out of the Gestapo building, this same car stood in front of the door. I even recognized the driver.

Particularly important in this whole period was a visit in 1939 by a well-known neurologist who, as Reich Education Director . . . was well up on Jewish matters. He told me, on two afternoons when we were alone, what would happen to me and my family along the lines of "Jews and friends of Jews must be exterminated. We are exterminating friends of Jews and all their offspring." Then he said that I could not be saved, but my family could. When I asked what I should do, he gave his answer in the form of a couple of stories in which the wife committed suicide and thereby saved her family. Then he asked: "How much Veronal [a sleeping pill] do you have?" When I answered, "Only two grams," he wrote me a prescription for the quantity that I was lacking. I carried the Veronal around with me for a few days, but then decided not to die, but instead to try to escape abroad with my family.

In four months, only three of my husband's colleagues dared to visit us. I was not allowed to go out during the day. When one evening I met a colleague's wife and complained that no friends or acquaintances had dared to visit me, she said: "That's not cowardice; we are just facing facts."[1]

Soon after, the family left Germany.

[1] Marie Kahle, in *The Night of Broken Glass: Eyewitness Accounts of Kristallnacht*, ed. Uta Gerhardt and Thomas Karlauf (Cambridge, UK: Polity Press, 2012), 88–90. Reproduced by permission from Polity Press.

READING

THOROUGHLY REPREHENSIBLE BEHAVIOR

Please note that this reading contains dehumanizing language. We have chosen to include it in order to honestly communicate the harmful language of the time; however, dehumanizing language should not be spoken or read aloud during class.

Wilhelm Kahle, Marie Kahle's eldest son, was a student at the University of Bonn. He was called before the university's disciplinary court for helping a Jewish storekeeper restore order to her shop after Kristallnacht. His "crimes" are spelled out in this "Disciplinary Judgment."

> The student of musicology Wilhelm Kahle will be punished, because of behavior unworthy of a student in regard to the protest action against Jewish businesses, by dismissal from the university and denial of credit for the semester's work.
>
> On 10 November 1938, there occurred in Bonn, as a result of the murder of the legation councilor vom Rath, a demonstration against Jews, in which the corset shop owned by the Jewess E. Goldstein was affected. On the late afternoon of 12 November 1938, the accused went with his mother to this shop, in which the latter had earlier made purchases. When they arrived at the shop, around 6 or 6:30 p.m., three Jewish females were leaving it. In the shop they met the owner and another Jewish person named Herz. The shop owner was busy putting boxes back on the shelves. After they had been there for about three minutes, Police Sergeant Peter Stammen entered the shop and wrote down the names of the Jewish persons and then also the name of the student Kahle's mother, and in doing so had some difficulties with the latter. He then turned to the student Kahle, who was putting the boxes that were on the counter back on the shelves, and asked him whether he was an interior decorator. The student said he was not, and then gave his name.
>
> Contrary to the charge, the Disciplinary Court has not been able to determine that the accused intended from the outset . . . to go to the Jewish shop. It is more of the opinion that no preconceived intention lay behind this visit, but rather that the visit took place only on the occasion of passing by the demolished shop. Further, the Disciplinary Court has not derived from the proceedings the impression that the student helped the Jewess put her merchandise back on the shelves but sees the student's actions simply as an effort, without any special intention, to help the Jewess in her work or to support her in some way.

Nonetheless, the student's behavior is thoroughly reprehensible. By finding it justifiable to enter a Jewish shop after the given incidents, he seriously endangered the reputation and dignity of the university and thereby violated his academic duties. Articles II and III of the Disciplinary Code for Students, 1 April 1935. He was to be penalized.

The accused's behavior requires a vigorous atonement. Since the accused seemed to be a little inept and awkward during the proceedings and was obviously under the influence of his mother, the Disciplinary Court has decided in mitigation merely to dismiss him from the university and deny him the credit for the entire semester's work.

In imposing this punishment, which is mild in relation to the offense, the Disciplinary Court has acted on the basis of the expectation that the student will pursue his further education at a greater distance from his parents' home, so that in the future he can mature into a more independent, more self-confident and more responsible person.[1]

[1] Uta Gerhardt and Thomas Karlauf, eds., *The Night of Broken Glass: Eyewitness Accounts of Kristallnacht* (Cambridge, UK: Polity Press, 2012), 90–91. Reproduced by permission from Polity Press.

READING

A VISITOR'S PERSPECTIVE ON KRISTALLNACHT

René Juvet, a Swiss merchant, was visiting friends in the countryside during the events of Kristallnacht. The next morning he drove to the town of Bayreuth, where he saw people watching as houses burned to the ground. At one point, he got out of his car to take a closer look at a crowd gathered in front of a warehouse where dozens of Jews were being held.

> I was reluctant to add myself to the assembled crowd but I had to see with my own eyes what was happening there. Through the great windows you could see perhaps fifty people in a bleak, empty hall. Most of them stood against the wall, staring gloomily, a few walked restlessly about, others were sitting—in spite of the severe cold—on the bare floor. Almost all of them, incidentally, were inadequately dressed; some only had thrown on a topcoat over their nightclothes. The SA people who had picked them up during the night had apparently not allowed them time to put on more clothing. Compared to what happened later, this was only a small beginning.

At the end of his description of Kristallnacht, Juvet writes:

> To the credit of my [non-Jewish German colleagues] I can report that they—with the exception of Neder, who took part in the operation in his role as an SA Führer—disapproved of the excesses. Some more, others less. Waldmeyer said nothing, but he was very thoughtful in ensuing days; Hoffmann, who could almost count himself as one of the old guard, made no attempt to conceal his horror from me. I also heard that the workers were outraged. . . .
>
> A little while after this I met our Nuremberg representative, a harmless and industrious person. He was a member of the SA but was, by chance, kept away from home that evening. . . .
>
> "I am happy I was not in Nuremberg that evening, it certainly would have rubbed me the wrong way," said our representative.
>
> I asked him whether he would have taken part if he had been there. "Of course," he said, "orders are orders."
>
> His words clarified a whole lot of things for me.[1]

[1] René Juvet, "Kristallnacht," in *Travels in the Reich, 1933–1945: Foreign Authors Report from Germany*, ed. Oliver Lubrich (Chicago: University of Chicago Press, 2010), 176–78.

READING
WORLD RESPONSES TO KRISTALLNACHT

Newspapers around the world reported on the events of Kristallnacht. The following story by Otto D. Tolischus of the *New York Times* was typical of many.

> A wave of destruction, looting and incendiaries [fires] unparalleled in Germany since the Thirty Years War and in Europe generally since the Bolshevist revolution, swept over Greater Germany today as National Socialist cohorts took vengeance on Jewish shops, offices and synagogues for the murder by a young Polish Jew of Ernst vom Rath, third secretary of the German Embassy in Paris.
>
> Beginning systematically in the early morning hours in almost every town and city in the country, the wrecking, looting and burning continued all day. Huge but mostly silent crowds looked on and the police confined themselves to regulating traffic and making wholesale arrests of Jews "for their own protection."
>
> All day the main shopping districts as well as the side streets of Berlin and innumerable other places resounded to the shattering of shop windows falling to the pavement, the dull thuds of furniture and burning shops and synagogues. Although shop fires were quickly extinguished, synagogue fires were merely kept from spreading to adjoining buildings.[1]

People everywhere were outraged. As the archbishop of Canterbury, Cosmo Gordon Lang, wrote in a November 12 letter to the editor of the *London Times*, "There are times when the mere instincts of humanity make silence impossible." Thousands of Americans agreed. They showed their outrage at huge rallies held in support of German Jews. In reporting these events to Berlin, the German ambassador expressed a fear that such protests might jeopardize the agreement concerning the Sudetenland in Czechoslovakia.

Leaders in Britain and France were very careful in how they responded. When members of Britain's Parliament asked Neville Chamberlain to condemn the pogrom, he simply said that newspaper reports were "substantially correct." He also expressed "deep and widespread sympathy" for those who were "to suffer so severely" for the "senseless crime committed in Paris."[2]

Similar comments from French leaders led the editor of a newspaper called *La Lumière* to warn, "In the past, when we protested against massacres in Ethiopia, China, Spain, we were told, 'Silence! You are warmongering.' When we protested against the mutilation of Czechoslovakia, we were told 'Keep quiet! You are a war party.' Today, when we protest against the contemptible persecution of defenseless Jews and their wives and children, we are told, 'Be silent! France is afraid.'"[3]

Condemnation from leaders in the United States was broad-based and widespread. Clergymen of all faiths spoke out against the burning of synagogues; politicians of all parties—Republicans and Democrats, isolationists and interventionists—denounced the violence against Jews and their houses of worship. The only world leader to take a stand was President Franklin D. Roosevelt. On November 15, six days after the pogrom, he opened a press conference by stating, "The news of the last few days from Germany has deeply shocked public opinion in the United States. Such news from any part of the world would produce a similar profound reaction among American people in every part of the nation. I myself could scarcely believe that such things could occur in a twentieth-century civilization."

But Roosevelt's response had to take into account widespread isolationist and antisemitic feelings in his administration, in Congress, and in the country. At his press conference, Roosevelt announced that the United States was withdrawing its ambassador to Germany, but he did not offer to help the thousands of Jews who were trying desperately to leave the Third Reich.

[1] Otto D. Tolischus, "The Pogrom," *New York Times*, November 19, 1938.

[2] "Chamberlain Deplores Nazi Pogroms; Acts to Aid British Jews in Reich," *Jewish Telegraphic Agency*, November 14, 1938, accessed April 26, 2016, http://www.jta.org/1938/11/15/archive/chamberlain-deplores-nazi-pogroms-acts-to-aid-british-jews-in-reich.

[3] Quoted in Anthony Read and David Fisher, *Kristallnacht: The Unleashing of the Holocaust* (New York: Peter Bedrick Books, 1989), 155.

HANDOUT

THE RANGE OF HUMAN BEHAVIOR VOCABULARY TERMS

DIRECTIONS: Use the context clues in the sentence in the first column to predict the meaning of each underlined term, and write your definition in the center column. Leave the third column blank.[1]

SENTENCE	PREDICTED MEANING	ACTUAL MEANING
The perpetrator of the crime was caught not long after robbing the convenience store and fleeing on foot down the crowded street.		
The victim of bullying didn't want to go to school and instead crawled back into bed and pretended to be sick.		
Despite feeling a knot in her stomach while reading the hateful comments on her childhood friend's social media feed, the bystander put away her phone and headed to the gym for volleyball practice.		
After three days of reading the increasing number of homophobic comments and threats on his friend's blog, the upstander picked up his phone and texted: "You don't deserve this treatment."		

[1] Kelly Gallagher, *Deeper Reading: Comprehending Challenging Texts*, 4–12 (Portland, ME: Stenhouse Publishers, 2004), 77–78.

MAP

THE GROWTH OF NAZI GERMANY

Between 1933 and 1939, Greater Germany expanded significantly as a result of the Third Reich's annexations and conquests in eastern Europe.

Facing History and Ourselves

READING

COLONIZING POLAND

A Polish woman identified as "Mrs. J. K." described her expulsion from her home by the Nazis:

> On 17 October 1939, at 8 a.m., I heard someone knocking at the door of my flat. As my maid was afraid to open it, I went to the door myself. I found there two German gendarmes [police], who roughly told me that in a few hours I had to be ready to travel with my children and everybody in the house. When I said that I had small children, that my husband was a prisoner of war, and that I could not get ready to travel in so short a time, the gendarmes answered that not only must I be ready but that the flat must be swept, the plates and dishes washed and the keys left in the cupboards, so that the Germans who were to live in my house should have no trouble. In so many words, they further declared that I was entitled to take with me only one suitcase of not more than 50 kilograms [110 pounds] in weight and a small handbag with food for a few days.
>
> At 12 noon they came again and ordered us to go out in front of the house. Similar groups of people were standing in front of all the houses. After some hours waiting, military lorries [trucks] drove up and they packed us in one after the other, shouting at us rudely and also striking us. Then they took us to the railway station, but only in the evening did they pack us into [boxcars], the doors of which they then bolted and sealed. In these [cars], most of which were packed with forty people, we spent three days, without any possibility of getting out. I hereby affirm that in my [car] there were six children of under ten years of age and two old men, and that we were not given any straw, or any drinking utensils, that we had to satisfy our natural needs in the tightly packed [car], and that if there were no deaths in our transport it was only because it was still comparatively warm and we spent only three days on the journey. We were unloaded, half dead at Czestochowa [in the General Government part of Poland,] where the local population gave us immediate help, but the German soldiers who opened the truck exclaimed, "What! Are these Polish swine still alive?"[1]

[1] Quoted in *Nazism: A History in Documents and Eyewitness Accounts, 1919–1945*, vol. 2, ed. Jeremy Noakes and Geoffrey Pridham (New York: Schocken Books, 1988), 937–38.

READING

CULTURAL MISSIONARIES

Melita Maschmann, who was then in her early 20s and held a leadership position in the BDM (the German initials of the League of German Girls), was among the first to live and work in the Warthegau.

She recalled:

> My colleagues and I felt it was an honor to be allowed to help in "conquering" this area for our own nation and for German culture. We had all the arrogant enthusiasm of the "cultural missionary." . . .
>
> How could young people, in particular, fail to enjoy such a life? It is true that if one visited the eastern parts of the Warthegau it was impossible to imagine oneself to be standing on lost German soil which had simply to be reclaimed for the Reich. This country was Polish through and through. Hitler had not reclaimed it but conquered it in battle. We knew that might had triumphed over right there. In those days we should probably have agreed that "the right of the strongest" had triumphed in the struggle for Lebensraum [living space for "Aryans"]. . . .
>
> Our existence at that time was for us like a great adventure. . . . All through our childhood the lament over Germany's defeat in the First World War and her misery in the postwar years had never ceased. I believe that growing up in a country where people's minds are dominated by such a mood has a fateful effect. Young people do not want to be ashamed of their fatherland. They depend more than older people on being able to honor, admire and to love it.
>
> The fact that we were allowed to perform a kind of "colonization work" in "advanced posts" there healed the wounds which our sense of honor had suffered in our childhood and early youth. Germany required us not merely to do a job of work but to give our entire selves. This feeling rose on many occasions to a sensation of intoxication. . . .
>
> It goes without saying that in this situation we were inclined to romanticize our existence in the "front line," and developed much of the colonial's presumptuous arrogance towards the "stay at homes." . . .
>
> I was the first Reich German B.D.M. leader to be sent to the Warthegau, and for a long time I was the only one. It is true that I had no leadership task—I had simply come to Posen to run the press department for the Regional leadership of the Hitler Youth—but I quickly made close contact with the local . . . B.D.M. leaders and was drawn into their work.[1]

[1] Melita Maschmann, *Account Rendered: A Dossier on My Former Self* (London: Abelard-Schuman, 1965), 73.

HANDOUT

NOTES ON THE GROWTH OF NAZI GERMANY, 1933–1939

1. The Nazi ideology of "race and space" inspired their plans for Germany's expansion throughout Europe, their desire to acquire new "living space" for the so-called Aryan race.

2. In 1938, the Nazis took advantage of inaction from world leaders and annexed Austria and part of Czechoslovakia (known as the Sudetenland), two areas with a large number of people who considered themselves of German descent.

3. In 1939, Germany and the Soviet Union signed a nonaggression pact (an agreement not to attack each other) and divided up Poland and the Baltic countries between them.

4. In September 1939, Germany invaded Poland and quickly defeated the Polish army. This was the beginning of World War II.

5. Hitler issued the order: "Poland is to be depopulated and settled with Germans." Therefore, the Nazis divided Poland into two parts. One part (the General Government) was designated for Poles, who the Nazis believed were an inferior race to Aryans, and for Jews. The other part (the Warthegau) was adjacent to Germany and designated for "true Germans."

6. The Germans expelled hundreds of thousands of Poles, Jews, and Sinti and Roma from the Warthegau to the General Government and gave their homes and property to "Aryan" Germans. Jews were confined to ghettos.

READING

TAKE THIS GIANT LEAP WITH ME

Sonia Weitz was born in Kraków, Poland. She was 11 years old when her family and other Polish Jews were herded into ghettos by the Nazis. Of the 84 members of her extended family, she and her sister Blanca were the only survivors of years in ghettos and concentration camps during the Holocaust. At an early age, she turned to poetry to help her cope with her emotions. Years after the Holocaust, Weitz wrote the poem "For Yom Ha'Shoah." *Yom Ha'Shoah* is Hebrew for "Day of Holocaust Remembrance."

FOR YOM HA'SHOAH

Come, take this giant leap with me
into the other world . . . the other place
where language fails and imagery defies,
denies man's consciousness . . . and dies
upon the altar of insanity.

Come, take this giant leap with me
into the other world . . . the other place
and trace the eclipse of humanity . . .
where children burned while mankind stood by
and the universe has yet to learn why
. . . has yet to learn why[1]

[1] Sonia Schreiber Weitz, *I Promised I Would Tell* (Brookline, MA: Facing History and Ourselves, Inc., 2012), 66.

HANDOUT

PHASES OF THE HOLOCAUST

In the video *Step by Step: Phases of the Holocaust*, historian Doris Bergen divides the history of the Holocaust into four phases:

1. Planning and Propaganda: 1933–1939
Key events:

- German Jews and other so-called inferior races and people are isolated from the rest of the population.
- Germany rebuilds military in violation of Treaty of Versailles.
- German government attacks properties and lives on Kristallnacht.
- Nazi government prepares German public for war.

2. Expansion and Violence: September 1939 – June 1941
Key events:

- World War II begins with German invasion of Poland.
- Nazi violence expands into Poland and across Europe.
- Nazis establish ghettos and new concentration camps to imprison millions of Jews.
- Einsatzgruppen (mobile killing units) murder millions of Jews and other targeted groups in mass shootings in eastern Europe.
- Germany invades Soviet Union.

3. Dedication to Mass Killing: 1941–1944
Key events:

- Decision is made by Hitler and his advisors to annihilate all of the Jews in Europe.
- Six killing centers are established, where millions of Jews, Sinti and Roma, and other targeted groups are murdered in gas chambers. The most infamous killing center is Auschwitz.

4. Death Marches: January 1945 – May 1945
Key events:

- As Germany is losing the war, and the Soviets are pushing the German military west, killing centers and camps are closed or liberated.
- Nazis force prisoners from camps to march from eastern Europe toward Germany. Hundreds of thousands die along the way.

MAP

JEWISH GHETTOS IN EASTERN EUROPE

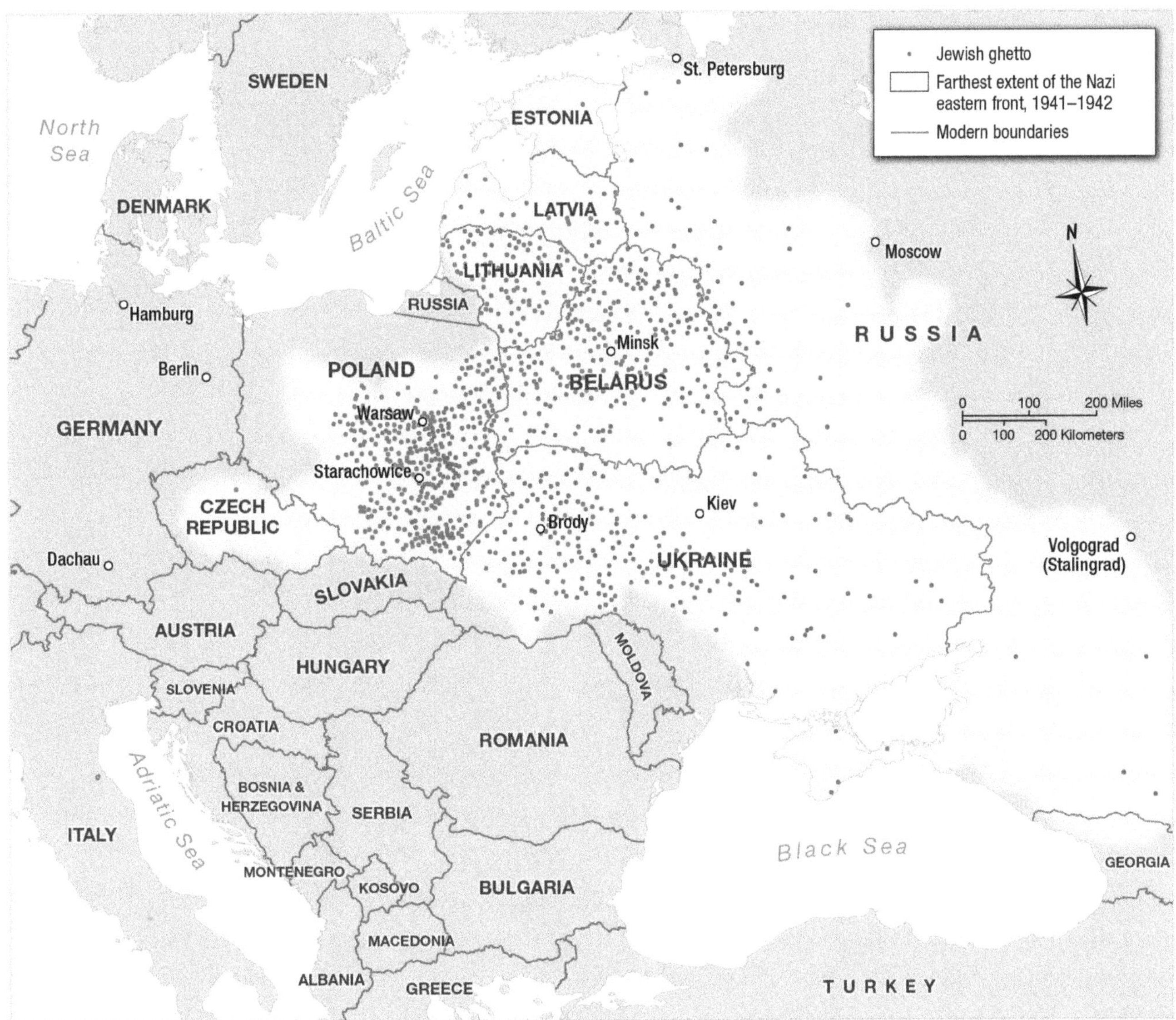

Historians estimate that about 1,100 Jewish ghettos were established by the Nazis and their allies in Europe between 1933 and 1945. This map shows the locations of the largest ghettos.

Facing History and Ourselves

MAP

MAIN NAZI CAMPS AND KILLING SITES

Between 1933 and 1945, the Nazis established more than 40,000 camps for the imprisonment, forced labor, or mass killing of Jews, Sinti and Roma, Communists, and other so-called "enemies of the state."

Facing History and Ourselves

IMAGE

THE BOY IN THE WARSAW GHETTO

This picture shows seven-year-old Tsvi Nussbaum in the Warsaw ghetto in 1943. The photo was taken by a Nazi photographer. There are conflicting accounts of whether this boy survived the war.

National Archives and Records Administration, College Park

READING
MOBILE KILLING UNITS

Physician Y. Kutorgene, who was not Jewish, witnessed the German invasion of her country, Lithuania. She wrote in her diary, "Thousands of people humiliated, without any protection, worse than animals, and that because they have 'other blood.'" On October 30, 1941, Dr. Kutorgene wrote about what had happened the previous day in the city of Kovno as the Nazis prepared to murder (by shooting) the Jews in the ghetto there:

> On [October 29] there was an announcement that everybody [every Jew] must come at six in the morning to the big square in the ghetto and line up in rows, except workers with the documents which were recently distributed to specialists and foremen. . . . The square was surrounded by guards with machine guns. It was freezing. The people stood on their feet all through that long day, hungry and with empty hands. Small children cried in their mothers' arms. Nobody suspected the bitter fate that awaited them. They thought that they were being moved to other apartments. . . . [There] was a rumor that at the Ninth Fort . . . prisoners had been digging deep ditches, and when the people were taken there, it was already clear to everybody that this was death. They broke out crying, wailed, screamed. Some tried to escape on the way there but they were shot dead. . . .[1]

[1] Y. Kutorgene, "Kaunaski Dnievnik (Kovno Diary) 1941–1942," *Druzhba Narodov* ("Amity of Nations"), VIII, 1968, 210–11, in *Documents on the Holocaust: Selected Sources on the Destruction of the Jews of Germany and Austria, Poland, and the Soviet Union*, ed. Yitzhak Arad, Israel Gutman, and Abraham Margaliot, trans. Lea Ben Dor (Lincoln and Jerusalem: University of Nebraska Press and Yad Vashem, 1999), 405–06.

READING
AUSCHWITZ

Auschwitz was a complex of camps where Jews, Sinti and Roma, prisoners of war, and Polish resisters were imprisoned and forced to perform slave labor. In October 1941, it also became the site of the largest killing center built by the Nazis.

This photograph shows Jewish women and children from Ukraine walking toward the gas chambers at Auschwitz, where they would be murdered.

United States Holocaust Memorial Museum, courtesy of Yad Vashem

Primo Levi, an Italian Jew, described his first few days as a prisoner in Auschwitz:

> Nothing belongs to us anymore; they have taken away our clothes, our shoes, even our hair; if we speak, they will not listen to us, and if they listen, they will not understand. They will even take away our name. . . . My number is 174517 . . . we will carry the tattoo on our left arm until we die.[1]

[1] Primo Levi, *Survival in Auschwitz* (New York: Touchstone, 1996), 26.

READING

WE MAY NOT HAVE ANOTHER CHANCE

Sonia Weitz was a young teenager in Poland when, in 1941, she and her family were forced to enter the Kraków ghetto. In 1943, Sonia, her older sister Blanca, and their father were sent to Płaszów, a slave-labor camp south of Kraków. In her book *I Promised I Would Tell*, she writes:

> Although men and women lived in separate parts of the camp, the two groups did manage to have contact with each other. For example, on one occasion I was sent to the ghetto with a cleanup detail. While there I found a jacket, a precious warm jacket. I smuggled it back to Płaszów to my father. It was comforting to think that the jacket would keep him warm that winter. On another day, I sneaked into my father's barracks on the other side of the barbed wire fence. While I was there, I met a boy who was about my age—14 or 15. The boy was playing a harmonica, an offense punishable by death. My father and I listened to the music, and my father said to me, "You and I never had a chance to dance together" . . . and so we danced. It is such a precious image, a bizarre and beautiful gift.[1]

Weitz and her sister were separated from their father soon after this moment. In December 1944, the two sisters were transferred to Auschwitz. They would never see their father again. The sisters were forced to march across Poland from Auschwitz to Bergen-Belsen, a concentration camp in Germany. They were later transferred to two other camps and at last liberated from Mauthausen, in Austria, in May 1945 by US troops.

[1] Sonia Schreiber Weitz, *I Promised I Would Tell* (Brookline, MA: Facing History and Ourselves, Inc., 2012), 35.

READING

DIARY FROM THE ŁÓDŹ GHETTO

In early 1942, a young girl living in the ghetto in Łódź (a Polish city) kept a diary of her experiences. Her name remains unknown, but her diary entries evoke the fear and suffering of life in the ghetto.

> [No Date]
>
> There is no justice in the world, not to mention in the ghetto . . . People are in a state of panic. And this hunger. A struggle against death from starvation. Life is terrible, living conditions are abominable, and there is no food . . .
>
> Wednesday March 11, 1942
>
> . . . Today I had a fight with my father. I swore at him, even cursed him. It happened because yesterday I weighed twenty decagrams of zacierki [egg noodles] and then sneaked a spoonful. When my father came back, he immediately noticed that some zacierki were missing. My father started yelling at me and he was right. But since the chairman [Mordechai Chaim Rumkowski, the head of the Jewish Council of Łódź] gave out these zacierki to be cooked, why can't I have some? I became very upset and cursed my father. What have I done? I regret it so much, but it can't be undone. My father is not going to forgive me. How will I ever look him in the eyes? He stood by the window and cried like a baby. Not even a stranger insulted him before. The whole family witnessed this incident. I went to bed as soon as possible, without dinner. . . . We would be a happy family, if I didn't fight with everybody. All the fights are started by me. I must be manipulated by some evil force. I would like to be different, but I don't have a strong enough will . . .
>
> Saturday March 14, 1942
>
> . . . O freedom! Will I have to stay behind this barbed wire forever? Will that sign be on the big board forever, [Entering Jewish residential area forbidden]? Will there always be a booth with a German guard who has a rifle on his shoulder? Has it always been like this? Will it stay like this? Oh, no! But who is going to live through it? I miss freedom. Especially on a warm sunny day. O sun! It's you who make me yearn for freedom. My heart is bleeding and my eyes are full of tears. Someone reading this in the future may sneer at me, say I'm an idiot . . .[1]

[1] Alexandra Zapruder, *Salvaged Pages: Young Writers' Diaries of the Holocaust* (New Haven: Yale University Press, 2002), 230–40.

READING

A BASIC FEELING OF HUMAN DIGNITY

Hanna Lévy-Hass was a Yugoslavian teacher imprisoned in the Bergen-Belsen concentration camp in Germany. She was held in a part of the camp for "exchange prisoners"—prisoners that the Nazis thought they might be able to exchange for Germans held prisoner by other countries. The exchange prisoners included many children.

Lévy-Hass wrote in her diary about both the loss of human dignity she and others suffered and how they sought to restore it.

> November 8, 1944
>
> I would love to feel something pleasant, aesthetic, to awaken nobler, tender feelings, dignified emotions. It's hard. I press my imagination, but nothing comes. Our existence has something cruel, beastly about it. Everything human is reduced to zero. Bonds of friendship remain in place only by force of habit, but intolerance is generally the victor. Memories of beauty are erased; the artistic joys of the past are inconceivable in our current state. The brain is as if paralyzed, the spirit violated.
>
> . . . We have not died, but we are dead. They've managed to kill in us not only our right to life in the present and for many of us, to be sure, the right to a future life . . .
>
> I turn things over in my mind, I want to . . . and I remember absolutely nothing. It's as though it wasn't me. Everything is expunged from my mind. During the first few weeks, we were still somewhat connected to our past lives internally; we still had a taste for dreams, for memories . . .
>
> November 18, 1944
>
> In spite of everything, my work with the children continues. . . . I cling desperately to every chance, however slight, to gather the children together to foster in them and in me even the slightest mental sharpness, as well as a basic feeling of human dignity.
>
> It was decided in the camp that Saturdays will be devoted to children's entertainment, mostly of a religious nature. In our barracks, we are also taking advantage of Saturdays to provide the children with some amusement, but adapted mostly to the overall mentality of the people here: oral recitations, singing solo or in chorus, small theatrical productions. Given the total lack of books, I collect and write down the material for these performances based on the children's memories and my own and more often than not, we must resort to improvising texts or poetic lines. A whole

throng of known tunes have been recovered thanks to the tireless efforts and concentration of all my students—but the words escape us as if they had been sucked into a pit. So we begin to invent lines, to rhyme, to create texts that affect us deeply, to invoke our distant homeland, glorious and heroic . . .

I carry out this task spontaneously, even instinctively I would say, through an irresistible need in my soul—in the rare moments when I manage to awaken it—and by an irresistible need that I can clearly sense coming from the children's souls. Because they take my lead, they get excited, they want to live, they want to rejoice, it's stronger than them. What heartbreak![1]

[1] Hanna Lévy-Hass and Amira Hass, *Diary of Bergen-Belsen*, trans. Sophie Hand (Chicago, IL: Haymarket Books, 2009), 85–88.

HANDOUT

CREATING A FOUND POEM

Creating a "found poem" from a Holocaust survivor's testimony can be a way to pay respectful attention to and honor his or her experiences. A found poem is one that is created using only words that have been copied and rearranged from another text.

DIRECTIONS: Use the following steps to create your poem:

1. Read the selected testimony at least two to three times. If possible, read it aloud at least once.

2. While reading the testimony one additional time, copy down at least 15 to 20 words or phrases from it that you find memorable or powerful.

3. Arrange the words and phrases you have selected into a poem. You might want to copy the words and phrases onto notecards or separate sheets of paper so that you can easily rearrange them. Try to arrange the words in a way that captures what you think is the essence of the testimony, as well as your experience of hearing it.

Here are a few more guidelines for creating your poem:

- You DON'T have to use all of the words and phrases you chose.
- You CAN repeat words or phrases.
- You CAN'T add other words besides those you copied from the testimony.
- Your poem DOESN'T have to rhyme.

4. When you are satisfied with your poem, give it a title.

READING

A COMMANDANT'S VIEW

In 1971, journalist Gitta Sereny interviewed Franz Stangl, who had been the commandant of the death camp at Sobibór and, later, the camp at Treblinka.

"Would it be true to say that you were used to the liquidations?"

He thought for a moment. "To tell the truth," he then said, slowly and thoughtfully, "one did become used to it."

"In days? Weeks? Months?"

"Months. It was months before I could look one of them in the eye. I repressed it all by trying to create a special place: gardens, new barracks, new kitchens, new everything: barbers, tailors, shoemakers, carpenters. There were hundreds of ways to take one's mind off it; I used them all."

"Even so, if you felt that strongly, there had to be times, perhaps at night, in the dark, when you couldn't avoid thinking about it."

"In the end, the only way to deal with it was to drink. I took a large glass of brandy to bed with me each night and I drank."

"I think you are evading my question."

"No, I don't mean to; of course, thoughts came. But I forced them away. I made myself concentrate on work, work, and again work."

"Would it be true to say that you finally felt they weren't really human beings?"

"When I was on a trip once, years later in Brazil," he said, his face deeply concentrated and obviously reliving the experience, "my train stopped next to a slaughterhouse. The cattle in the pens, hearing the noise of the train, trotted up to the fence and stared at the train. They were very close to my window, one crowding the other, looking at me through that fence. I thought then, 'Look at this; this reminds me of Poland; that's just how the people looked, trustingly, just before they went into the tins . . .'"

"You said tins," I interrupted. "What do you mean?" But he went on without hearing, or answering me.

". . . I couldn't eat tinned meat after that. Those big eyes . . . which looked at me . . . not knowing that in no time at all they'd all be dead." He paused. His face was drawn. At this moment he looked old and worn and sad.

"So you didn't feel they were human beings?"

"Cargo," he said tonelessly. "They were cargo." He raised and dropped his hand in a gesture of despair. Both our voices had dropped. It was one of the few times in those weeks of talks that he made no effort to cloak his despair, and his hopeless grief allowed a moment of sympathy.

"When do you think you began to think of them as cargo? The way you spoke earlier, of the day when you first came to Treblinka, the horror you felt seeing the dead bodies everywhere—they weren't 'cargo' to you then, were they?"

"I think it started the day I first saw the Totenlager [death camp] in Treblinka. I remember [Christian Wirth, the man who set up the death camps] standing there next to the pits full of blue-black corpses. It had nothing to do with humanity —it couldn't have; it was a mass—a mass of rotting flesh. Wirth said, 'What shall we do with this garbage?' I think unconsciously that started me thinking of them as cargo."

"There were so many children; did they ever make you think of your children, of how you would feel in the position of those parents?"

"No," he said slowly, "I can't say I ever thought that way." He paused. "You see," he then continued, still speaking with this extreme seriousness and obviously intent on finding a new truth within himself, "I rarely saw them as individuals. It was always a huge mass. I sometimes stood on the wall and saw them in the tube. But—how can I explain it—they were naked, packed together, running, being driven with whips like . . . " The sentence trailed off.

. . . "Could you not have changed that?" I asked. "In your position, could you not have stopped the nakedness, the whips, the horror of the cattle pens?"

"No, no, no. This was the system. . . . It worked. And because it worked, it was irreversible."[1]

[1] Gitta Sereny, *Into that Darkness: An Examination of Conscience* (London: Pan Books, 1977), 200–02. Reproduced by permission of the Estate of Gitta Sereny and The Sayle Literary Agency.

READING

BYSTANDERS AT HARTHEIM CASTLE

While the Nazis loudly proclaimed the campaigns to demonize and isolate Jews and "Gypsies" (the name Germans gave to two ethnic groups known as the Sinti and Roma) in newspapers and magazines, on billboards, and over the radio, they attempted to keep secret the program to murder mentally and physically disabled "Aryans." And yet by the end of 1940, most Germans were aware of some if not all aspects of the killings.[1] As historian Gordon J. Horwitz investigated the history of Mauthausen, a small Austrian town 90 miles from Vienna, he uncovered evidence of what the residents of a nearby village had known about the "euthanasia," or medical killing, program taking place there.

Soon after Austria became part of the Third Reich in 1938, the Germans built a labor camp for political prisoners in Mauthausen. As the camp expanded, German officials took over buildings in a number of nearby villages. One of those buildings was Hartheim Castle, which was a home for mentally handicapped children. In researching the history of Hartheim Castle, Horwitz discovered a letter written by a man he identified as "Karl S." The letter recalls events in 1939.

> [The] house of my parents was one of the few houses in Hartheim from which one could observe several occurrences. After Castle Hartheim was cleared of its inhabitants (around 180 to 200 patients) in the year 1939, mysterious renovations began which, to an outsider, however, one could hardly divine, since no [local] labor was used for it, and the approaches to the castle were hermetically sealed. Following completion of the renovation work, we saw the first transports come and we could even recognize some of the earlier residents who showed joy at returning to their former home.[2]

Karl S. watched the buses arrive from a window in his father's barn. He recalled that groups of two or three buses came as frequently as twice a day. Soon after they arrived, "enormous black clouds of smoke streamed out of a certain chimney and spread a penetrating stench. This stench was so disgusting that sometimes when we returned home from work in the fields we couldn't hold down a single bite."[3]

A woman called Sister Felicitas, who had formerly worked with children kept in the castle, had similar memories:

> My brother Michael, who at the time was at home, came to me very quickly and confidentially informed me that in the castle the former patients were burned. The frightful facts which the people of the vicinity had to experience first hand, and the terrible stench of the burning gases, robbed them of speech. The people suffered dreadfully from the stench. My own father collapsed unconscious several times, since in the night he had forgotten to seal up the windows completely tight.[4]

Horwitz notes, "It was not just the smoke and stench that drew the attention of bystanders. At times human remains littered parts of the vicinity. In the words of Sister Felicitas, 'when there was intense activity, it smoked day and night. Tufts of hair flew through the chimney onto the street. The remains of bones were stored on the east side of the castle and in ton trucks driven first to the Danube [River], later also to the Traun.'"[5]

As evidence of mass murders mounted, Christian Wirth, the director of the operation, met with local residents. He told them that his men were burning shoes and other "belongings." When they asked about the strong smell, he told them it came from a device that turned old oil and oil byproducts into a water-clear, oily fluid that was of "great importance" to German submarines. Wirth ended the meeting by threatening to send anyone who spread "absurd rumors of burning persons" to a concentration camp.[6] The townspeople took him at his word. They did not break their silence.

The castle at Hartheim was one of six facilities, most of which were hospitals, that the Nazis outfitted with gas chambers and ovens in 1940 and 1941 in order to murder physically and mentally disabled people and burn their remains. Between May 1940 and May 1941, 18,269 patients were murdered at Hartheim.[7]

[1] Carol Poore, *Disability in Twentieth-Century German Culture* (Ann Arbor: University of Michigan Press, 2007), 87.

[2] Quoted in Gordon J. Horwitz, *In the Shadow of Death: Living Outside the Gates of Mauthausen* (New York: Free Press, 1990), 59.

[3] Quoted in Horwitz, *In the Shadow of Death: Living Outside the Gates of Mauthausen*, 59.

[4] Quoted in Horwitz, *In the Shadow of Death: Living Outside the Gates of Mauthausen*, 60.

[5] Quoted in Horwitz, *In the Shadow of Death: Living Outside the Gates of Mauthausen*, 60–61.

[6] Quoted in Horwitz, *In the Shadow of Death: Living Outside the Gates of Mauthausen*, 61–62.

[7] Robert N. Proctor, "Culling the German Volk," in *How Was It Possible? A Holocaust Reader*, ed. Peter Hayes (Lincoln: University of Nebraska Press, 2015), 267.

READING

PROTESTS IN GERMANY

By 1942, people living in Germany were increasingly aware of the mass murders in places to the east.

Some of the first Germans to speak out against Nazi injustices were a group of students at the University of Munich. In winter 1942, Hans Scholl, his sister Sophie, and their friend Christoph Probst formed a small group known as the White Rose. Hans, a former member of the Hitler Youth, had been a soldier on the eastern front, where he witnessed the mistreatment of Jews and learned about deportations. In 1942 and 1943, the White Rose published four leaflets condemning Nazism. The first leaflet stated the group's purpose: the overthrow of the Nazi government. In the second leaflet, the group confronted the mass murders of Jews:

> We do not want to discuss here the question of the Jews, nor do we want in this leaflet to compose a defense or apology. No, only by way of example do we want to cite the fact that since the conquest of Poland three hundred thousand Jews have been murdered in this country in the most bestial way. Here we see the most frightful crime against human dignity, a crime that is unparalleled in the whole of history. For Jews, too, are human beings—no matter what position we take with respect to the Jewish question—and a crime of this dimension has been perpetrated against human beings.[1]

In February 1943, the Nazis arrested the Scholls and Probst and brought them to trial. All three were found guilty and were guillotined that same day. Soon afterward, others in the group were also tried, convicted, and beheaded.

In March 1943, German author Friedrich Reck-Malleczewen wrote in his diary:

> The Scholls are the first in Germany to have had the courage to witness for the truth. . . . On their gravestones let these words be carved, and let this entire people, which has lived in deepest degradation these last ten years, blush when it reads them: . . . "He who knows how to die can never be enslaved." We will all of us, someday, have to make a pilgrimage to their graves, and stand before them, ashamed.[2]

Although the Nazis were able to destroy the White Rose by executing its members, they could not keep its message from being heard. Helmuth von Moltke, a German aristocrat, smuggled the group's leaflets to friends in neutral countries. They, in turn, sent them to the Allies, who made thousands of copies and then dropped them over German cities. As a lawyer who worked for the German Intelligence Service, von Moltke had been aware of the murders for some time but had taken no action. By late October, he was asking, "May I know this and yet sit at my table in my heated flat and have tea? Don't I thereby become guilty too?"[3]

1 "The Second Leaflet," The White Rose Society, accessed May 24, 2016, http://www.whiterosesociety.org/WRS_pamphets_second.html.

2 Friedrich Reck-Malleczewen, *Diary of a Man in Despair*, trans. Paul Rubens (New York: Collier Books, 1970), 179–81.

3 Helmuth James von Moltke, *Letters to Freya, 1939–1945*, ed. and trans. Beate Ruhm von Oppen (New York: Knopf, 1990), 175.

READING
DECIDING TO ACT

In 1942, Marion Pritchard was a graduate student in German-occupied Amsterdam. She was not Jewish, but she observed what was happening to the Jews of her city. One morning, while riding her bicycle to class, she witnessed a scene outside an orphanage for Jewish children that changed her life:

> The Germans were loading the children, who ranged in age from babies to eight-year-olds, on trucks. They were upset, and crying. When they did not move fast enough the Nazis picked them up, by an arm, a leg, the hair, and threw them into the trucks. To watch grown men treat small children that way—I could not believe my eyes. I found myself literally crying with rage. Two women coming down the street tried to interfere physically. The Germans heaved them into the truck, too. I just sat there on my bicycle, and that was the moment I decided that if there was anything I could do to thwart such atrocities, I would do it.
>
> Some of my friends had similar experiences, and about ten of us, including two Jewish students who decided they did not want [to] go into hiding, organized very informally for this purpose. We obtained Aryan identity cards for the Jewish students, who, of course, were taking more of a risk than we were. They knew many people who were looking to . . . "disappear," as Anne Frank and her family were to do.
>
> We located hiding places, helped people move there, provided food, clothing, and ration cards, and sometimes moral support and relief for the host families. We registered newborn Jewish babies as gentiles . . . and provided medical care when possible.

The decision to rescue Jews often led to other difficult choices. Pritchard described what happened when she agreed to hide a Jewish family:

> The father, the two boys, and the baby girl moved in and we managed to survive the next two years, until the end of the war. Friends helped take up the floorboards, under the rug, and build a hiding place in case of raids. . . . One night we had a very narrow escape.
>
> Four Germans, accompanied by a Dutch Nazi policeman came and searched the house. They did not find the hiding place, but they had learned from experience that sometimes it paid to go back to a house they had already searched, because by then the hidden Jews might have come out of the hiding place. The baby had started to cry, so I let the children out. Then the Dutch policeman came back alone. I had a small revolver that a friend had given me, but I had never planned to use it. I felt I had no choice except to kill him. I would do it again, under the same circumstances, but it still bothers me. . . . If anybody had really tried to find out how and where he disap-

> peared, they could have, but the general attitude was that there was one less traitor to worry about. A local undertaker helped dispose of the body, he put it in a coffin with a legitimate body in it. . . .
>
> Was I scared? Of course, the answer is "yes." . . . There were times that the fear got the better of me, and I did not do something that I could have. I would rationalize the inaction, feeling it might endanger others, or that I should not run a risk, because what would happen to the three children I was now responsible for, if something happened to me, but I knew when I was rationalizing.

In reflecting on her choices and those made by others during the war, Pritchard was troubled by a "tendency to divide the general population during the war into a few 'good guys' and the large majority of 'bad guys.' That seems to me to be a dangerous oversimplification . . . The point I want to make is that there were indeed some people who behaved criminally by betraying their Jewish neighbors and thereby sentencing them to death. There were some people who dedicated themselves to actively rescuing as many people as possible. Somewhere in between was the majority, whose actions varied from the minimum decency of at least keeping quiet if they knew where Jews were hidden to finding a way to help when they were asked."

[1] Carol Rittner and Sondra Myers, eds., *The Courage to Care: Rescuers of Jews During the Holocaust* (New York: New York University Press, 1986), 29. Reproduced by permission from New York University Press.

[2] Rittner and Myers, *The Courage to Care*, 29–31.

[3] Rittner and Myers, *The Courage to Care*, 32–33.

READING

LE CHAMBON: A VILLAGE TAKES A STAND

All over Europe, a small number of individuals tried to save Jews. But in Le Chambon, a village in southern France, the entire community became involved in rescue. Le Chambon was a Protestant village in a predominantly Roman Catholic region, which before and even during the war was a center of tourism. Now its residents turned their tiny mountain village into a hiding place for Jews from every part of Europe. Between 1940 and 1944, Le Chambon and other nearby villages provided refuge for more than 5,000 people fleeing Nazi persecution, about 3,500 of whom were Jews.[1] Magda Trocmé, the wife of the local minister, explained how it began.

> Those of us who received the first Jews did what we thought had to be done—nothing more complicated. It was not decided from one day to the next what we would have to do. There were many people in the village who needed help. How could we refuse them? A person doesn't sit down and say I'm going to do this and this and that. We had no time to think. When a problem came, we had to solve it immediately. Sometimes people ask me, "How did you make a decision?" There was no decision to make. The issue was: Do you think we are all brothers or not? Do you think it is unjust to turn in the Jews or not? Then let us try to help![2]

Almost everyone in the community of 5,000 took part in the effort. Even the children were involved. When a Nazi official tried to organize a Hitler Youth camp in the village, the students told him that they "make no distinction between Jews and non-Jews. It is contrary to Gospel teaching."[3]

The majority of the Jewish refugees were children. The villagers provided them with food, shelter, and fake identity papers. They also made sure that those they sheltered were involved as much as possible in the life of the town, in part to avoid arousing suspicion from other visitors. Whenever residents of Le Chambon learned of an upcoming police raid, they hid those they were protecting in the surrounding countryside. The values of the village were perhaps expressed best by its minister, André Trocmé, who concluded his sermons with the words, "You shall love the Lord your God with all your heart, with all your mind and with all your strength and love your neighbor as yourself. Go practice it."[4]

In February 1943, the police arrested André Trocmé and his assistant, Edouard Theis. Although they were released after 28 days, the Gestapo continued to monitor their activities. In summer 1943, the Gestapo offered a reward for André Trocmé's capture, forcing him into hiding for ten months. Many knew where he was, but no one turned him in.[5]

Historian Marianne Ruel Robins notes:

> The fact that an entire community participated (or watched and said nothing) is remarkable indeed. The silence observed by the people of the Plateau was an

> important condition for its success, not simply because it sheltered Jews from external threats, but also because it minimized internal dissent. To refrain from talking meant that one would not shame one's neighbor for his lack of participation; it also meant that different rationales for behavior would not conflict with another, be they commitment to pacifism, nationalism, Christian charity or judeophilia. Silence did not necessarily imply that everyone implicitly agreed on the reasons for hiding Jews, but rather that most people came to agree that something ought to be done.[6]

The rescuers of Le Chambon also drew support from people in other places. There was an extensive network of sympathizers throughout the region who could be called upon for help with communication and organization. Jewish rescue organizations brought Jewish children to the area for protection. Church groups, both Protestant and Catholic, helped fund their efforts. So did the World Council of Churches. Also, a group known as the Cimade led hundreds of Jews across the Alps to safety in Switzerland.

When Magda Trocmé reflected on her choices years after the war, she said, "When people read this story, I want them to know that I tried to open my door. I tried to tell people, 'Come in, come in.' In the end I would like to say to people, 'Remember that in your life there will be lots of circumstances where you will need a kind of courage, a kind of decision on your own, not about other people but about yourself.' I would not say more."[7]

1 "Le Chambon-sur-Lignon," United States Holocaust Memorial Museum, last modified January 2016, accessed May 17, 2016, https://www.ushmm.org/wlc/en/article.php?ModuleId=10007518.

2 Carol Rittner and Sondra Myers, eds., *The Courage to Care: Rescuers of Jews During the Holocaust* (New York: New York University Press, 1986), 102. Reprinted by permission from New York University Press.

3 Philip Hallie, *Lest Innocent Blood Be Shed* (London: Michael Joseph, 1979), 102.

4 Hallie, *Lest Innocent Blood Be Shed*, 170.

5 "Le Chambon-sur-Lignon," United States Holocaust Memorial Museum, http://www.ushmm.org/wlc/en/article.php?ModuleId=10007518.

6 Marianne Ruel Robins, "A Grey Site of Memory: Le Chambon-sur-Lignon and Protestant Exceptionalism on the Plateau Vivarais-Lignon," *Church History* 82, no. 2 (2013).

7 Rittner and Myers, *The Courage to Care*, 107.

READING

DENMARK: A NATION TAKES ACTION

By 1943, anyone in German-occupied Europe who wanted to know was aware of what was happening to Jews. For a variety of reasons—including fear, self-interest, passivity, and even sympathy with German policies—few in occupied nations acted to protect Jewish residents. Many government officials in the occupied countries turned over documents that allowed Germans to quickly identify Jews, and local police often helped Germans find and arrest those Jews. The exception was in Denmark.

After the Germans conquered Denmark in 1940, Hitler had allowed the pre-war government to stay in power and kept only a token military force in the nation. German policy regarded Danes as members of a superior race, similar to Germans. Nevertheless, the Danes deeply resented the occupation of their country, and some fought back with acts of sabotage, riots, and strikes. In summer 1943, the Nazis decided to retaliate. They limited the power of King Christian X, forced the pre-war Danish government to resign, and disbanded the Danish army. They also ordered the arrest of a number of Christian and Jewish leaders.

A few weeks later, the Danes learned that the Germans were planning to deport the nation's entire Jewish population. That news came from Georg Ferdinand Duckwitz, a German diplomat in charge of overseeing shipping between Germany and Denmark. In the early 1930s, Duckwitz was drawn to the Nazis' ultranationalist propaganda and joined the party. However, as Hitler's violent intentions came to light, he became disillusioned with the party. And when the Germans took over Denmark, he sympathized with the hardships and challenges of the Danish people. When Duckwitz learned in late September of secret orders to prepare four cargo ships for transporting Danish Jews to Poland, he immediately passed on the information to leaders in the Danish resistance. They, in turn, informed the Danish people.

When leaders of the Danish church were told of the Germans' plan, they sent an open letter to German officials. On Sunday, October 3, 1943, that letter was read from every pulpit in the nation.

> Wherever Jews are persecuted because of their religion or race it is the duty of the Christian Church to protest against such persecution, because it is in conflict with the sense of justice inherent in the Danish people and inseparable from our Danish Christian culture through the centuries. True to this spirit and according to the text of the Act of the Constitution all Danish citizens enjoy equal rights and responsibilities before the Law and full religious freedom. We understand religious freedom as the right to exercise our worship of God as our vocation and conscience bid us and in such a manner that race and religion per se can never justify that a person be deprived of his rights, freedom or property. Our different religious views notwithstanding, we shall fight for the cause that our Jewish brothers and sisters may preserve the same freedom which we ourselves evaluate more highly than life itself.[1]

The Danes responded in the following weeks with a plan to keep Jews from being deported by hiding them until they could be evacuated to nearby Sweden, a neutral nation. It was a collective effort—organized and paid for by hundreds of private citizens, Jews and Christians alike. Fishermen, many of whom could not afford to lose even one day's pay, were paid to transport the Jews to Sweden. The money was also used for bribes. It was no accident that all German patrol ships in the area were docked for repairs on the night of the rescue.

Not every Jew was able to leave. Some were captured as they waited for a boat, while others were picked up at sea. But, in the end, the Nazis were able to deport only 580 of Denmark's 7,000 Jews to the Terezín camp-ghetto, and the Danish government constantly inquired about their status. No Danish Jews were shipped to a death camp, and with the exception of a few who died of illness or old age in Terezín, all of them returned safely to Denmark after the war.

[1] Quoted in Leo Goldberger, ed., *The Rescue of the Danish Jews: Moral Courage Under Stress* (New York: New York University Press, 1988), 6–7.

HANDOUT

PERPETRATORS, BYSTANDERS, UPSTANDERS, AND RESCUERS

DIRECTIONS:

1. Read the story out loud together, pausing at the end of each one- to two-paragraph section to annotate *choices*, *consequences*, and *questions*. There will be sections of the text with no choices or consequences, so every paragraph won't necessarily have an annotation.

    • Write *choice* in the margin alongside any moments where the individual, group, or nation faced a decision and made a significant choice.

    • Underline information in the text that helps you understand what might have led the individual, group, or nation to make those choices.

    • Write *consequence* in the margin alongside any moments where the story discusses the possible or actual consequences for the individual, group, or nation's choices.

2. Discuss the questions below and record your group's answers on this handout. The information you gather today will help you prepare your presentation in the next lesson.

Reading Title: ____

1. Where does your reading take place?

2. What are the significant choices discussed in your reading? Who made them?

3. What reasons or explanations did each individual, group, or nation give for their choices?

4. What were the possible (or actual) consequences of these choices for the individual, group, or nation? In other words, what did the individual(s) know could happen if they made this choice, and/or what actually did happen to them as a consequence of making the choice?

5. How do you think the individual, group, or nation in this reading defined its universe of obligation?

6. What were the impacts of the choices?

7. In this unit, you have learned about the range of human behavior in times of crisis and heard stories about *survivors*, *resisters*, *perpetrators*, *bystanders*, *upstanders*, and now *rescuers*. It is important to understand that individuals and groups don't fit neatly into one category, even when talking about a single event, and that during the Holocaust, there was a range of choices available at any given moment, although this range was more limited in the 1940s than in earlier decades, especially in Germany, Austria, and Poland.

Where on the range of behavioral categories (see list above) does your reading's individual, group, or nation fall, and why? (Remember that they could fall into more than one category.) What makes you say that?

HANDOUT

CHOICES AND CONSEQUENCES

Name of the individual, group, or nation making the choice	What was one choice that they made?	What were the possible motivations for the choice? Did the individual telling the story give a possible explanation or reason for the choice?

My questions:

What were the possible (or actual) consequences for the choice?	Label the action(s): perpetrator, bystander, upstander, rescuer

HANDOUT

JUSTICE AFTER THE HOLOCAUST ANTICIPATION GUIDE

DIRECTIONS: The statements below represent some of the main issues that the Allies faced as they tried to figure out how to achieve justice after World War II and the Holocaust.

Read each statement in the left column. Decide if you **strongly agree (SA)**, **agree (A)**, **disagree (D)**, or **strongly disagree (SD)** with it. Circle your response and provide a one- to two-sentence explanation of your opinion (on separate paper if needed).

STATEMENT	YOUR OPINION
1. It is possible to achieve justice for the crimes committed during the Holocaust.	**SA** **A** **D** **SD** Explain:
2. The victors in a war have the right to punish the defeated countries however they wish.	**SA** **A** **D** **SD** Explain:
3. Those responsible for the Holocaust should be immediately killed or jailed; they do not have the right to a fair trial in a court of law.	**SA** **A** **D** **SD** Explain:
4. Bringing perpetrators to justice in courts is an effective way to prevent future crimes.	**SA** **A** **D** **SD** Explain:

STATEMENT	YOUR OPINION
5. Since each country has its own laws, citizens should be brought to trial by the courts of their own country. It is unfair for some nations, or the international community, to impose their laws on citizens of other nations.	**SA** **A** **D** **SD** Explain:
6. Bystanders allowed the Holocaust to happen. If more people had stood up rather than looking the other way, millions of lives could have been saved. The bystanders should be punished along with the perpetrators.	**SA** **A** **D** **SD** Explain:
7. Spreading hateful lies that influence people to harm others is a crime against humanity.	**SA** **A** **D** **SD** Explain:
8. The only person responsible for the Holocaust was Adolf Hitler. Nazi leaders were following the laws of their country and the orders of their elected leader. They should not be punished.	**SA** **A** **D** **SD** Explain:

HANDOUT

AN OVERVIEW OF THE NUREMBERG TRIALS

DIRECTIONS: Below are eight descriptions of key events from the Nuremberg trials. Read each description, and then choose one or more statements from the "Justice after the Holocaust Anticipation Guide" that relate to the event. Write the statement number (1–8) from the anticipation guide on the line after the event to which it relates. Then, in the space provided on this handout, explain the connection that you see between the two.

1. Soviet Premier Joseph Stalin suggested executing 50,000 members of the German army. Winston Churchill, the British leader, thought that high-ranking Nazi leaders should be hanged. But other leaders thought they should go to trial.

Statement #: ___________

2. The Allied countries agreed to put Nazi leaders on trial for two reasons: 1) to punish those responsible, and 2) to prevent future crimes against humanity. Those who organized the trials wanted future leaders to know that if they acted like Hitler and other Nazi leaders, they would be punished for their actions; they could not just get away with murdering their own citizens.

Statement #: ___________

3. Beginning in November 1945, an international trial—a court case involving many countries—was held in the city of Nuremberg in Germany, so the trials were called the Nuremberg trials. The trials included judges and lawyers from each of the winning countries (Britain, France, the United States, and the Soviet Union). The Nazi defendants also had lawyers to defend them. Some argued that it was unfair for the Allied powers to bring the Nazis to trial because they had not broken any laws. (At this point in time, there were no international laws forbidding a government from murdering its own citizens.)

Statement #: ___________

4. Twenty-four men were indicted (charged with a crime) during the first set of trials at Nuremberg. These defendants included military leaders, Nazi Party leaders, and officers who worked at the concentration camps. Hitler and several other Nazi leaders were not indicted because they had committed suicide or escaped at the end of the war. Some lower-ranking officers, soldiers, and bureaucrats who participated in the Holocaust were indicted in later trials. Bystanders also were not put on trial at Nuremberg or in future trials.

Statement #: ___________

5. The defendants in the first set of trials were charged with four types of crimes. One of these crimes was "crimes against humanity." One of the men charged with crimes against humanity was Julius Streicher. He was minister of propaganda of the Nazi Party. He was responsible for spreading hateful lies about Jews in the newspaper and in other forms, such as children's books.

Statement #: ___________

6. Many Nazis charged with "crimes against humanity" argued that they were only following orders and that they had not broken any laws by their actions.

Statement #: __________

7. Nineteen of the defendants were found guilty in the first Nuremberg trial. Twelve were sentenced to death by hanging. Three were given life in prison, and four were given prison terms ranging from 10 to 20 years. In the three years that followed, many more trials of Germans were held in Nuremberg. By 1949, more than 200 German officials, including the highest-ranking surviving Nazi leaders, members of the *Einsatzgruppen* mobile killing units, and dozens of physicians and industrialists, were brought to trial for their roles in the war and in the mass murder of civilians. The vast majority were convicted and sentenced to death or given prison sentences of varying lengths.

Statement #: __________

8. After the war, the Allied powers also had to consider what Germany should do to "pay back" the survivors of the Holocaust and the families of the victims. After all, the Nazis had taken all of their money and property and had caused immeasurable suffering. A program was set up to provide money (reparations) to those who could prove they were victims of the Nazis, and Germany was supposed to give back stolen property to its rightful owners (if they were still alive).

Statement #: __________

9. After you have finished discussing each section and making connections to the anticipation guide, work together to complete a 3-2-1 activity, described below, that you will share in a class discussion.

A. Write three things you learned about the Nuremberg trials and the complexities of seeking justice after World War II and the Holocaust after reading this overview.

B. Write two questions that your group has about the Nuremberg trials and the complexities of seeking justice after World War II and the Holocaust after reading this overview.

C. Write one idea from this overview that you found particularly interesting or confusing (you can do this one individually).

HANDOUT

INTRODUCTION TO POST–WORLD WAR II HUMAN RIGHTS INSTITUTIONS

DIRECTIONS: As you are reading, annotate the text by completing the following steps:

1. Circle words that are unfamiliar.
2. Put a question mark (?) in the margin in places where you feel confused.
3. Answer the questions that follow the text.

The United Nations:

In the midst of World War II, even as they struggled to defeat Germany and Japan, leaders of the Allied nations were also beginning to envision a new international institution that would replace the failed League of Nations and ensure global peace and cooperation once the war ended. In the immediate aftermath of the war, they established this. The Charter of the United Nations was signed on June 26, 1945, by leaders from 50 nations. Today, the UN is made up of 192 countries whose purpose is to help solve problems related to human rights, military conflicts, and economic development. The United Nations adopts treaties, resolutions, and conventions, and, in doing so, establishes international law.

The Universal Declaration of Human Rights:

The devastation of World War II encouraged the creation of a system of principles that could ensure the protection of basic human rights and dignity. Eleanor Roosevelt, the widow of President Franklin Delano Roosevelt, was one of the first American delegates to the United Nations. She worked with a small group of representatives from countries around the world to define the most essential universal rights (including the right to a fair and public trial, the right to belong to a religion, and the right to education) and establish them in an official document.

The United Nations approved the declaration in 1948, but the work was only partially done. The Universal Declaration of Human Rights (UDHR) itself was not binding: no part of the document could be enforced legally. Roosevelt had hoped that the UDHR would become a treaty, and every nation that ratified the treaty "would then be obligated to change its laws wherever they did not conform to the points contained in the covenant." The commission thought a treaty might be worked out within the next few years, but this hope proved to be too optimistic. The work to secure human rights around the world remains an ongoing struggle.

The Convention on the Prevention and Punishment of the Crime of Genocide:

On December 9, 1948, the United Nations adopted the Convention on the Prevention and Punishment of the Crime of Genocide, often called the Genocide Convention, which classified genocide as a crime under international law. By the 1950s, a sufficient number of countries had ratified the convention, and it entered into force (although the United States did not ratify it until 1986).

The International Criminal Court:

Enforcement of international laws like the Genocide Convention remained a problem because there was no permanent international court empowered to bring charges against violators. After mass violence, "ethnic cleansing," and genocide took place in Yugoslavia and Rwanda during the 1990s, two temporary courts were created by the United Nations Security Council to bring perpetrators to trial.

The temporary nature of the international courts, along with continued violence around the world, raised several questions: Was it possible to create a more permanent international criminal court? In 1998, a permanent International Criminal Court (ICC) was established, with jurisdiction over the most important international crimes, including genocide. Since its establishment, the ICC has opened investigations of crimes in ten countries, including Uganda, Sudan (for the situation in Darfur), the Democratic Republic of Congo, Libya, and the Central African Republic. It has convicted two Congolese warlords of war crimes and crimes against humanity.

Many powerful nations, including the United States, China, India, and Russia, do not participate in the ICC. Many countries feared that signing the treaty would undermine their sovereignty and make them vulnerable to outside interference in their affairs. They were also reluctant to expose their citizens, especially those in the military, to prosecution by the ICC.

IMAGE

ROHINGYA REFUGEES ARRIVING BY BOAT, 2017

Refugees arrive on the Bangladesh side of the Naf River on October 1, 2017, after fleeing their village in Myanmar.

Kevin Frayer / Getty Images

HANDOUT

EVIDENCE CHART

INITIAL CLAIM	
What is your opening claim about the choices of individuals, groups, and nations that led to the Holocaust?	

EVIDENCE	
What evidence do you have from the sources you investigated to support your initial claim? Make sure to cite your sources.	

DOUBLE CHECK	
What ideas from the sources contradict your claims? Have you forgotten anything? Make sure to cite your sources.	

HANDOUT

SAMPLE COUNTERARGUMENT WORKSHEET

WORD BANK

Useful language to use when making and refuting counterarguments

Nevertheless	Some might believe	But	Even so	Despite
On the one hand	On the other hand	While	It is true	Yet
In contrast	To some extent	Although	Admittedly	However
It might seem that	What this argument fails to account for			

1. Argument This thesis is true because . . .	
2. Counterargument Yet some people argue . . .	
3. Refutation But . . .	
4. Response On the other hand . . .	

HANDOUT

OUTLINING YOUR ESSAY: GRAPHIC ORGANIZER FOR BODY PARAGRAPH

OUTLINE FOR BODY PARAGRAPH #: ________

THESIS (The purpose of my paper is to prove . . .)

ARGUMENT (This thesis is true because . . .)

Evidence to support argument (with citation):	**Analysis:** This evidence supports my argument because . . .
1.	
2.	
3.	

(optional)

COUNTERARGUMENT (Some people argue . . .)

Evidence to support argument (with citation):	**Analysis:** This evidence supports my argument because . . .
1.	
2.	
3.	

IMAGE

UDHR INFOGRAPHIC

THE UNIVERSAL DECLARATION OF

HUMAN RIGHTS

Adopted by the General Assembly of the United Nations in 1948, the Universal Declaration states fundamental rights and freedoms to which all human beings are entitled.

You have the responsibility to respect the rights of others.

We are all born free and equal.

Everyone is entitled to these rights no matter your race, religion, sex, language, or nationality.

Everyone has the right to life, freedom, and safety.

No one can take away any of your rights.

No one has the right to hold you in slavery.

No one has the right to torture you.

You have a right to be recognized everywhere as a person before the law.

We are all equal before the law and are entitled to equal protection of the law.

You have the right to seek legal help if your rights are violated.

No one has the right to wrongly imprison you or force you to leave your country.

You have a right to a fair, public trial.

Everyone is innocent until proven guilty.

You have the right to privacy. No one can interfere with your reputation, family, home, or correspondence.

You have the right to travel.

You have the right to seek asylum in another country if you are persecuted in your own.

Everyone has the right to a nationality.

All consenting adults have the right to marry and to raise a family.

You have the right to own property.

Everyone has the right to belong to a religion.

You have the right to think and voice your opinions freely.

Everyone has the right to gather as a peaceful assembly.

You have the right to participate in the governance of your country, either directly or by helping to choose representatives in free and genuine elections.

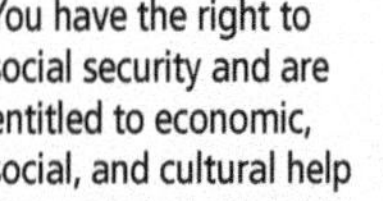

You have the right to social security and are entitled to economic, social, and cultural help from your government.

Every adult has the right to a job, a fair wage, and membership in a trade union.

You have the right to leisure and rest from work.

Everyone has the right to an adequate standard of living for themselves and their family.

Everyone has the right to an education.

Everyone has the right to freely participate in the culture and scientific advancement of their community, and their intellectual property as artist or scientist should be protected.

We are all entitled to a social order in which we may enjoy these rights.

Everyone's rights and freedoms should be protected unless they obstruct the rights and freedoms of others.

No State, group, or person can use this Declaration to deny the rights and freedoms of others.

This is a simplified version of the UDHR. For the complete text, visit www.un.org

The Universal Declaration of Human Rights was adopted by the UN General Assembly in 1948. It states the basic rights and freedoms to which all people are entitled.

SHARING OUR LEARNING: WRITING CONNECTIONS

WRITING CONNECTION 1
(DAY 5)

How can "single stories" influence a society's universe of obligation?

DIRECTIONS: Write an evidence-based claim about some ways in which "single stories" influence a society's universe of obligation.

WRITING CONNECTION 2
(DAY 8)

Which aspects of the German government and society during the years of the Weimar Republic strengthened democracy, and which aspects weakened it?

DIRECTIONS: Complete the graphic organizer on page 51 ("The Bubbling Cauldron") to represent the impediments and opportunities for democracy during the Weimar period.

WRITING CONNECTION 3
(DAY 10)

What role did individuals and groups play in the destruction of democracy in Germany?

DIRECTIONS: Create a pie chart to represent the distribution of responsibility for that transformation between the following groups: Adolf Hitler, President Hindenburg, members of the Reichstag, German citizens, and other historical actors you deem significant.

WRITING CONNECTION 4
(DAY 13)

How did the Nazis attempt to build a "racially pure and harmonious national community"? What were the roles of laws, propaganda, the media, arts, and education?

DIRECTIONS: Create an annotated list of three pieces of evidence that show how the Nazis attempted to build a "racially pure and harmonious national community."

WRITING CONNECTION 5
(DAY 15)

What roles can individuals, groups, and nations who are not targeted by violence and terror play in perpetuating or preventing injustice?

DIRECTIONS: Respond to this question in an argumentative paragraph that uses evidence from Day 1 and Day 2 of the Kristallnacht lesson.

WRITING CONNECTION 6
(DAY 20)

What choices did individuals, groups, and nations make in response to the events of the Holocaust? What factors influenced their choices to act as perpetrators, bystanders, upstanders, or rescuers?

DIRECTIONS: Give an oral presentation on the choices that individuals, groups, and nations made in response to the events of the Holocaust.

FINAL WRITING CONNECTION & TAKING INFORMED ACTION

Essential Question: How did the choices of individuals, groups, and nations lead to the Holocaust?

WRITING PROMPT

In an essay, students will construct an argument that addresses the essential question using specific claims and relevant evidence from historical and contemporary sources while acknowledging competing views.

INFORMED ACTION

In a hands-on project, students will apply lessons gained from their study of the Holocaust to their own communities. The informed action has three parts:

UNDERSTAND: In groups of three to five students, research the universal rights and responsibilities in the Universal Declaration of Human Rights (UDHR), which arose, in part, as an effort to prevent another global calamity on the scale of the Holocaust.

ASSESS: In the same groups, consider how the UDHR applies to your community (e.g., your school, neighborhood, or some other community to which you belong). Pick a right from the UDHR that you believe is particularly meaningful and/or not fully achieved in your community. Use the "levers of power" framework to do the following:

- Identify a group or individual who has power over addressing the human right that you identify (e.g., your peers, the media, elected officials, nonprofit organizations)
- Determine what message you think they most need to hear related to the UDHR/your identified issue
- Decide on a medium to effectively communicate your message to your intended audience

ACT: Disseminate your group's chosen right through a medium of your choice (e.g., a mini-exhibition, mural, video documentary, podcast, zine, spoken word poem, or blog post). Be sure to illustrate or explain why that right has particular resonance for your community. In addition, your medium and message should be tailored to appeal to an individual or group with power over your chosen issue.

www.ingramcontent.com/pod-product-compliance
Lightning Source LLC
Jackson TN
JSHW071521160125
77248JS00007B/17

* 9 7 8 1 9 4 0 4 5 7 3 8 3 *